D1203754

WILLIAM BRICE

REVELATORY NATURE

WILLIAM BRICE

REVELATORY NATURE

Foreword by
Peter Goulds
Introduction by
Kimberly Davis
With an essay by
Howard N. Fox
Chronology by
Bonnie Earls-Solari
and John Brice

L | A | LOUVER

FOREWORD

Peter Goulds

When I was recruited by the University of California, Los Angeles to become a visiting lecturer in the Design area of the Art Department, I was 24 years of age, full of enthusiasm, and a little green behind the ears, to say the least. Although William Brice was a faculty member in Fine Art, he was the first colleague to lend a hand. We met in the department's office, and he proceeded to take the time to show this young English lad around campus, and to guide me through the potential entanglements of political life in academia.

Bill Brice and I became professional friends, and between 1972–1975, we served on several faculty and graduate student committees together. I learned a great deal from Bill and other colleagues, such as Elliot Elgart, Sam Amato and Charles Garabedian, in the Fine Art Department; with John Neuhart, Mitsuru Kataoka, Fred Marcus and Bill Brown in the Design Area; and Karl Werkmeister, Carlo Pedretti and Tim Clark in Art History. This was a time of great change at UCLA, under Chancellor Charles E. Young's leadership. William Brice was absolutely instrumental in helping to shape UCLA's Fine Art Department into the world-class, studio-based academic school for which it has been widely recognized during these past 25 years.

As my own research at UCLA as an information designer evolved, and in large measure, due to my exposure to and expanding interest in the studio activities of artists working in Southern California, I decided that an art gallery could become a form through which I would be able to embrace the increasing breadth and scope of my interests in 20th century art. Bill Brice always attracted the leading art dealers of his day—Frank Perls in Los Angeles; Charles Alan in New York; and with Frank's demise, the up-and-coming new art dealer of that time in L.A., namely, Nicholas Wilder.

William Brice in his studio, 1952

L.A. Louver was formed during the summer of 1975, and with Nick's retirement from art dealing in 1980, the baton to represent Bill's work was handed over into my care, and to Robert Miller, in New York. A full cycle was underway, and now I would be working on behalf of William Brice, the artist. A small measure of his kindness and consideration could be repaid, and how more fortunate could a young art dealer be than to represent such an important painter. Our director, Kimberly Davis, joined L.A. Louver in 1985. In his later years, Kimberly very much took Bill under her wing, and provided him with the careful attention and meaningful dialogue that all artists look for, and rightfully require, from those individuals fortunate enough to represent their interests, outside the sanctity of the studio, and in the world at large.

Two years ago, Bill died, preparing for a supper party with a small group of artist friends that he was to host at home with Shirley. Bill cooked, and the best martinis would have been administered by Bill's careful hand, stirred, not shaken.

With important museum exhibitions of Bill's work presented at the Los Angeles County Museum of Art, Museum of Contemporary Art and the Hammer Museum, all of which were accompanied by superb scholarship: What other useful study and commentary could be provided regarding Bill, his work, and the unique contribution he made to artistic practice in the U.S.?

In reflecting upon our predicament, a suggestion was made that perhaps Howard Fox, with his new station in life as curator emeritus of contemporary art, Los Angeles County Museum of Art, might have the time to provide a fresh insight into Bill's work, particularly since it had evolved since MOCA's survey exhibition in 1986. Howard's essay in this catalogue is, quite simply stated, superb, and he is to be congratulated for

Peter Goulds, William Brice and Frances Brody at L.A. Louver, 1984

this significant contribution to Brice scholarship. Howard's text, and this book, provide the stimulus for, and herald the need to experience, a new look at this important artist, and a full and complete retrospective of William Brice's work. In thinking about and assembling a direction for this exhibition, Kimberly Davis, together with Bill's son, John Brice, and myself, were aided in our task by the registration support of Lisa Wells, who provided remarkable care and dedication to the accounting of over 11,000 works, mostly executed on paper, and often in the form of "notations," which remained in Bill's studio at the time of his death. From this documentation, it became clear that from within the estate, Bill's developing ideas as an artist could be very particularly described through a selection of 30 drawings from 1960-1985, and that we would be able to document Bill's full achievement as an artist within the framework of a well-illustrated catalogue.

A brilliant chronology written by Bonnie Earls-Solari and John Brice, and edited by our Managing Director, Lisa Jann, aims to tell the colorful story of Bill's life and work. Our Archivist Alice Flather's diligence and dedication is evident throughout these pages, in the photography and illustrations she was able to secure. Together with our designer, Stefan Bucher of 344 Design, all of these individuals have brought together this most imaginative, well-presented publication. We are also grateful to Antonia Bostrom, Merritt Price, Cherie Chen and Jacklyn Burns of the Getty; Julie Green and Richard Schmidt of David Hockney Studio; Cindy Burlingham of the Grunwald Center for the Graphic Arts; Charlotte Brown of the UCLA University Archives; Phyllis Diebenkorn, and Richard Grant and Rakia Faber of the Diebenkorn Foundation; and Kathan Brown, Valerie Wade and Sasha Baguskas of Crown Point Press, for their generosity and contributions to this undertaking.

L.A. Louver is very proud to have represented the artist William Brice from 1980 –
2009, and we are extremely grateful to Bill's wife, Shirley, his son, John, and his
grandson, Saxon (who assisted his grandfather in his studio during his later years),
for granting us permission to mount this show, and produce this catalogue. It has
been a privilege to bear witness to the generosity of the Brice Family and all involved
in L.A. Louver's memorial exhibition and publication, honoring William Brice.
Their spirit gratefully resides in this project for Bill, whose independent stance as
an artist flew in the face of artistic adversity, and bucked the urges to conform
to the contemporary fashion of his time. Yet he remained the most open-minded
individual toward the impulses and gyrations of what has to be the living,
breathing, contemporary art of our time. William Brice was very much of his
time and place, in 20th century American art history.

Peter Goulds
Founding Director
L.A. Louver / Rogue Wave Projects
September 2010

INTRODUCTION
Kimberly Davis

"Elegant" is the first word that comes to mind when I think about Bill Brice. It wasn't just his imposing physical presence that made everyone look up to him. He was respected for his refined manner, his extraordinary wit, his intelligence and charm, and especially for his ability to make everyone around him feel comfortable. He would listen, reflect and respond with great clarity and insight. He was a brilliant teacher, particularly influential at UCLA, and his teaching made a huge impression on the Los Angeles artistic community. He was a great friend to many artists, and counted Richard Diebenkorn among his closest friends. He was also at home in Hollywood's social world through his mother, Fanny Brice, and his sister and brother-in-law, Fran and Ray Stark.

Bill had a long and distinguished professional career before I met him in 1985 at L.A. Louver. His work has been placed in many major museums, including the Hirshhorn Museum and Sculpture Garden, the Museum of Modern Art, and the Los Angeles County Museum of Art. He's had important exhibitions at the San Francisco Museum of Modern Art, the Santa Barbara Museum of Art, the Dallas Museum of Art, and LACMA. L.A. Louver and Robert Miller worked closely to facilitate the retrospective exhibition at the Museum of Contemporary Art in 1986, which traveled to the Grey Art Gallery in New York. This exhibition was very well received, and set the stage for other institutions to acquire his paintings, including MOCA, the Orange County Museum of Art, the San Diego Museum of Contemporary Art, and the Carnegie Museum in Pittsburgh.

In 1993, an exhibition of prints and drawings was curated by the Grunwald Center for the Graphic Arts that created a better understanding of Brice's practice.

Untitled, 1978
oil on canvas
117 x 93 in. (297.2 x 236.2 cm)

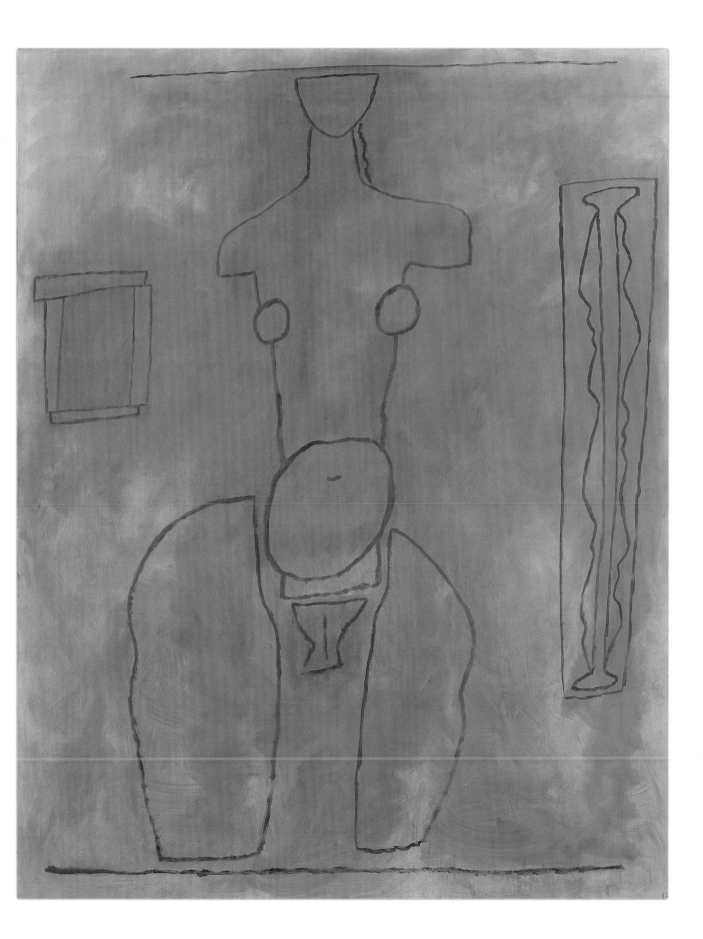

Untitled, 2005
ink on paper
24 x 18 in. (61 x 45.7 cm)

As he worked, Bill edited many drawings that didn't meet his standards, filing them in drawing pads. A catalogue raisonné of prints was included in the catalogue, which incorporated all the prints he produced with Tamarind, Crown Point Press, and various small editions he created as books with his writer friends.

Our exhibitions at L.A. Louver were extremely successful: paintings in 1984, drawings in 1989, watercolors in 1990, and a final beautiful painting exhibition in 1998. In the last 15 years of his life, his studio practice was very private, and almost no one was allowed to visit. But every day that he could, Bill visited the studio to draw. He refined the same compositions endlessly, working towards perfection. When he got it right, it was obvious—the drawings were elegant.

In the last year of his life, Bill promised me that he was "almost done" with a new painting, and we scheduled a small exhibition in my office, along with a series of related drawings. We even ordered the frame. But after his death, I visited the studio to find the painting nowhere near completion. However, the beginnings of an elegant composition were suggested through an overlay of ideas on tracing paper. Drawings on top of the painting showed a new direction. Cutout forms suggested that, like Matisse late in his life, he was establishing a new working method. But with the exception of a couple of drawings, there were only some notations that hinted at the work he had hoped to create.

I had the enlightening opportunity to review all the drawings that remained in the studio—and there were thousands. But Bill had done a pretty good editing job, so our task of determining what he might have allowed to leave the studio was easy. I went through every scrap of paper, and was delighted to come to a fuller understanding of his working process. His constant refinement did, in fact, yield the best work.

There are many exhibitions that can and will be made from Bill's work, but for this memorial exhibition, we wanted to show William Brice at his most elegant and refined. The memory of him and his work will always be strong for us at L.A. Louver, and we are honored to have the opportunity to present this exhibition and catalogue.

Kimberly Davis
Director
L.A. Louver

"The legacy of art is a record of man's experience;
a vision of his mind and soul; his appetites, aspirations,
fears, dreams, delights and beliefs. In light of this,
an essential value of painting is that of revelation, and
the implication for the painter is that there is something
to be revealed and someone to reveal it to.

"Art is creative for the sake of realization. Painting needs
to serve as a work of faith, of passionate involvement
and conviction. The endurance of a painting is dependent
upon its continuing pertinence to life; its utility
should be considered in terms of its revelatory nature."

William Brice
St. Louis Museum of Art
1964

REVELATORY
NATURE

REVELATORY NATURE
THE ART OF WILLIAM BRICE
Howard N. Fox

If there is such a thing as an "artist's artist," William Brice is one such. When that description is invoked, it usually connotes an artist dedicated, perhaps against the odds or against fashionability—and often hazarding the risk of career impediments—to a highly individual aesthetic, yet realizing that aesthetic with virtuosic finesse and aplomb, all the while earning and enjoying the earnest admiration of other artists, who may be the subject's primary audience. There is a faintly wistful notion of going it alone—admirably so—imbedded in the term's usage, as if being an "artist's artist" were notionally inflected with a spirit of self-sacrifice, as of one having given up something desirable—fame, perhaps, and commensurate fortune—in the noble pursuit of a singular inspiration. If there is a nearly ineffable tinge of melancholy about the term, it nonetheless remains a title conferred by peers with the utmost respect and regard.

Who was this inspired artist who, for whatever reasons, went it alone? The literature surrounding Brice's achievement is oddly scant on his personal history. (The biographical timeline included in this catalogue, compiled by the artist's son, John Brice, and Bonnie Earls-Solari, should serve to flesh out the record.) The basics are well known, and are outlined by Richard Armstrong in his 1986 catalogue essay for the exhibition *William Brice: A Selection of Painting and Drawing, 1947-1986* presented by the Museum of Contemporary Art, Los Angeles. William Brice was born in New York in 1921, the son of Broadway, radio and film star, Fanny Brice, and Jules "Nicky" Arnstein, whose relationship was the inspiration for the heavily fictionalized Broadway musical *Funny Girl* and its film adaptation (both produced by Fanny Brice's son-in-law, and William Brice's brother-in-law, Ray Stark).

He grew up in various well-appointed homes on Manhattan's Upper East Side, and enjoyed the privileges of a wealthy household: a lustrous social life with frequent visits by luminaries from the theater and music worlds specifically, and the arts in general; governesses and private tutors; a summer home, vacations, travel. Young Brice showed a precocious interest in art, and was strongly encouraged by his mother to pursue that interest; she retained painter Henry Botkin to foster the boy's artistic inclinations. She also supported his interest in other artists; at age 14, the lad acquired a 1906 drawing by Picasso, the first of numerous works he would collect by other artists over the years. Later, in 1938, when the Brices moved to Los Angeles so that Fanny Brice could pursue her radio and film career, William was enrolled in the Cumnock School for Expression. In 1940, he traveled back to New York briefly to take classes at the Art Students League, returning later that year to Los Angeles, and eventually graduating from Chouinard Art Institute, then the city's premier art school, in 1942.

But the family's privileged circumstance was not without troubles during young Brice's formative years. As his son John has commented, "He was born with a silver spoon rammed down his throat."[1] The governesses who attended to him, and his tutor Henry Botkin, largely served as parental figures or surrogates, during his youth. As a hugely popular stage and radio personality, his mother was rarely "between projects," and toured frequently in shows across the country, sometimes being away from home for weeks at a time. When she was in New York, she usually worked nights, socialized afterward, and often did not return home until very late at night. As John Brice observed about his father's home life as a boy, "Even when Fanny was around, she wasn't around, and I think he missed her presence." Moreover, life with his father was less than satisfying. "Nick Arnstein," John reported of the grandfather he never really knew, "was an immensely stylish man who did not believe in gainful employment to

---

1 — Unless otherwise noted, citations to John Brice are from unrecorded discussions with the author in Spring and Summer 2010.

support the finesse of his lifestyle." He was a gambler who had ties to the so-called "Jewish mafia," and was prone to shady dealings. In one of the most notorious financial scandals of the era, in 1924, Arnstein was convicted of securities fraud and sentenced to three years in federal prison. He was not at all close to young Bill and his sister Frances to begin with, and then he was incarcerated. Fanny Brice divorced him soon after his release from prison, and he had little regular contact with the family thereafter. John Brice surmises that the absence of a father "left Bill a haunted man throughout his life."

As for William Brice, John says that while his father was frank with about his family life and background, he mostly kept his more haunted thoughts to himself and his therapist. John describes his father's life as "compartmentalized": on the one hand, he would often enjoy a great bonhomie among his many friends (who continue to speak avidly about his sophistication, social graces and deep generosity) and celebrate life with a robust sense of abandon; yet he rarely opened up about whatever heartache he harbored, remaining private before friends and family, and forever silent about his inner self.

Except for his ideas about art. On that count, John Brice describes his father as an "art priest," passionately devoted to its ideals. In a typewritten manuscript of lecture notes, William Brice, sounding priestly indeed, wrote, "The legacy of art is [a] record of man's experience, his relation to [his] environment, his aspirations, fears, dreams, delights and beliefs. In the light of this an essential value of painting is that of revelation. Appreciation of art demands recognition of its revelatory nature."[2] Brice lectured frequently on the nature of art, both as a public speaker at many museums and as a teacher in the studio art program at University of California, Los Angeles, where he was on the faculty from 1953 until he retired in 1991. He was, and remains, a fabled teacher. Perhaps his idealism about art and its wellsprings was never more abundant than with his students: Brice began the first class of each semester by announcing to his assembled students, "I am not your teacher." After a silent moment before his perplexed charges, he clarified: "You are your teacher," explaining that he saw his responsibility as guiding and nurturing them in their individual quests, each for their own artistic flourishing. Revelation, he counseled, begins internally with each person, and it is the true artist's mission, or calling, to communicate one's deepest insights, feelings and intuitions with the world through the nearly mystic associative powers of art.

Brice's own innermost feelings, expressed through obscure narratives, or non-narratives, comprise an introspective, often melancholy, oeuvre. Among his earliest post-student works from the mid- and late 1940s are a group of striking series of *Rock Compositions*— still-lifes—of small rocks and stones depicted as highly formalized arrangements on a floor or a table against a wall. These painted stones, though inspired by real stones that washed ashore and were collected by Brice on walks along the Pacific coast, are all well worn by time, and smoothed into irrefutably biomorphic shapes that almost resemble human torsos or other body parts—bones, internal organs, male and female erogenous zones. The grouped stones variously touch and overlap, caressing one another, reclining one atop another, or resting in partial isolation from the others. It is as if they are not merely occupying space and volume, but are *behaving*. It is virtually impossible to look at these depictions without reading them, even if at some subliminal level, as being about entities in relationship—not merely a formal relationship—to one another. These "scenes" have a peculiar, palpable intensity—a theatricality, really—as if they were silent psychodramas in which the stones are acting out some murky roles. Which is to say that Brice imbues these still-lifes with a tacit anthropomorphism, prompting the viewer to perceive them as an allegory of human relationships, both physical and psychological. These exquisite arrangements are further aestheticized by an odd, milky white light that suffuses the space and makes them seem suspended in time, much as with the meditative quietude of a still-life by Giorgio Morandi or the near metaphysical stillness of a Zurbarán still-life. Uncanny as it might seem to vest objects as lifeless as stones with a sense of inner psychological drama, Brice attempts and succeeds at doing so in these works that, in retrospect, presage important attributes of his "totemic" works decades later.

Sea Rocks, 1947
oil on canvas, 18 $^{1}/_{16}$ x 28 $^{3}/_{16}$ in. (45.8 x 71.6 cm)
Collection of the University of Michigan Museum of Art
Gift of Mr. and Mrs. Roy R. Neuberger (1962/2.6)

To the extent that these *Rock Compositions* deal with subjects in nature, they have some slight affinity with landscape painting, and for a time in the early 1950s, Brice took an interest in painting the environs of Los Angeles, which then were considerably less developed than today. Big homes and gated communities now roost on what still counted as wilderness—though a somewhat citi-

Ocean and Rocks, 1954–55
oil on board, 64 x 80 in. (162.6 x 203.2 cm)
Collection of the San Diego Museum of Art
Gift of Mary Grant Price and Vincent Price, Jr.

fied wilderness—just a few decades earlier. Brice's landscapes, as well as a related body of flower paintings, executed at the same time as the ascent of abstract expressionism, are among the most abstract works he ever made. Despite his remoteness from New York (where he did journey with some frequency), Brice was not unsusceptible to the compelling ideas and challenges of abstract expressionism that were invigorating American and international artists.

Yet even in his most inflected and abstracted works, strong suggestions of representational elements abide. Thus in a work like, say, *Land Fracture* (1954–55) in the collection of the University of California, Los Angeles, Hammer Museum, whose tortured painterly forms defy easy representational

Land Fracture, 1954–55
oil and sand on masonite,
96 x 72 in. (243.8 x 182.9 cm)
Collection of the University of California,
Los Angeles, Hammer Museum
Gift of Mr. and Mrs. Ray Stark

Mottled Things, 1954, oil on texture board, 55 $^7/_8$ x 18 in. (139.7 x 45.7 cm)
Collection of the Santa Barbara Museum of Art

identification, there are clear aspects of landscape painting: a chunky rock-like
formation, the branch of a tree, patches of blue sky and white clouds. Similarly,
Mottled Things (1954) in the collection of the Santa Barbara Museum of Art, verges
on illegibility as a depiction, yet there are clear references to rock formations and other
mottled *things*, as the title indicates. Brice's impulse to abstraction is always grounded
in representation, much as were some of the more radical experiments of early cubism:
Picasso's *The Architect's Table* (1912) in the collection of New York's Museum of
Modern Art, for example, whose extreme faceting verges on nearly "illegible" visual
display for its own formal sake, is nonetheless recognizably and resolutely
a traditional still-life—albeit one rendered in a revolutionary visual vocabulary.

In an interview for *View*, an irregularly published journal based in San Francisco, Brice commented that "I've never had an inclination towards descriptive illusionism, per se, toward the literal recording of perceptual appearance. Nor have I ever been a nonobjective painter," [3] preferring to root his art in stylized pictorial representation. Though there were many major mid-century modernists who emphatically combined robust abstraction with representational painting (such as Willem de Kooning with his fiercely painted women, or Arshile Gorky with his dream-like, surrealist-inflected imagery), in the main, they were primarily abstractionists who used recognizable images as a foundation upon which to "push paint"—to create gestural paintings and handle the medium of oil paint in a physical, at times acrobatic,

3 — "Interview: Part I" by Wendy Diamond, Crown Point Press, San Francisco, December 1985; reprinted in View, Vol. IV, No. 6, Spring 1988, p. 6, Point Publications, San Francisco.

display of passionate control over dynamic energy. Brice by contrast—himself a true sophisticate of painterly technique and of draftsmanship—seems always more compelled by *pictures* and our ache to discover their obscure meanings in the hungering human psyche. Painting and drawing per se mattered deeply to Brice, but not so much as *what* he painted or drew. Brice's insistence on treading the perceptual ambiguity between representation and abstraction imbues his art with a profound yet lyrical aesthetic tension—a tension born of the incomprehensibility of what we, as viewers, most want to comprehend about human experience. Brice plumbs and probes the psychological depth of the very desire for "meaning" and "comprehension." His target is as much the mind's eye as the seeing eye, and pictures—icons, pictograms, portraits— always served as his conduit.

Brice's foray into gestural, painterly abstraction was, then, a temporary—though bold and fruitful—venture, a successful experiment. But his interest in landscape and abstraction did not disrupt or displace his love of making figurative art. Many of his concurrent works from Brice's "middle period," roughly from the mid-1950s and well into the 1960s, were figure studies and moody meditations on the female nude, and they would become omnipresent in his oeuvre to the very end—but in a very different form. Clearly these nudes were of deep psychological importance to the artist, both an inspiration and a preoccupation, perhaps even a fixation. As early as 1953, in an unpublished note to himself from that year, while drawing images of nature on Mulholland Ridge, and reflecting specifically on the sounds of nature—"the crackle of the motion of the bug, the ant"—Brice concluded with an especially sensual, erotic afterthought: "There are so many other forms and movements thrilling to me, the sounds of thighs and shoulders, breasts, the articulation of hands and stance of legs and back. Soft billow—the pillow of warm flesh of the stomach, of the buttocks, of the pear and the peach—the clear water of the mouth and of the apple."[4] Just as in this diaristic passage, his reflections on nature gave forth to an erotic reverie, so did the landscape elements of his earlier paintings and drawings yield to his passion for the female form.

The great majority of his pictures from this period were female nudes, with an occasional male nude making an appearance. They were usually contemplative, solitary figures in vague interiors or walking in a garden. These women are often shadowy presences— less like individuals with distinctly portrayed faces and a visible sense of character (though Brice occasionally did make some very striking portraits) than somewhat ghostly, phantom-like presences in isolation. Even when they appear with others, such as the nude male and female couple in a garden in the painting *Two Figures* (1965–66), they really are not paired at all, but are rather isolated from one another, each in their own space on opposite sides of the composition, separated pictorially by a tree trunk.

The female resides close to the picture plane, while the male seems almost reclusive, deep in the recessed picture space. There is no clear situation, no identifiable characters, no discernable action in this tableau, yet the composition itself confers a poignant narrative full of longing.

Two Figures, 1965–66
oil on canvas
80 x 96 in. (203.2 x 243.8 cm)
Private collection

4 — Unpublished manuscript, 1953; collection of the Estate of William Brice.

By the late 1960s, Brice, now nurturing a newfound interest in both early and late Matisse, began incorporating a brighter palette into his paintings and works on paper, and a flatter approach to modeling his figures. The pastel drawing *Reclining Figure with Blue and Green Pond* (1967) reveals a summary sense of depiction, a shallow, compressed pictorial space, and an abbreviated interest in detail. By now, Brice's formal approach to making pictures was changing. They were becoming flatter, more frontal, and highly structured—almost as if an invisible geometry were governing the composition, independent of what it depicted. Though his devotion to the female nude remained the basis of his art, Brice began to grant himself license to render more abstractly. Some of the images began to look like the markings of a prehistoric cave painting, something akin to pictograms or hieroglyphs. In 1968, he first incorporated images of compound rock formations that occur in nature, as well as fragments of ancient Greek architecture.

Reclining Figure with Blue and Green Pond
1967, pastel on paper
23 ³/₄ x 18 ³/₄ in. (60.3 x 47.6 cm)

right: Untitled, 1978
oil on canvas, 72 x 96 in.
(182.9 x 243.8 cm)
Collection of the Museum of
Contemporary Art San Diego

Then in 1970, Brice went to Greece with his wife Shirley and son John. The encounter with antiquity was revelatory: as art historian David Acton explains, "At that time, the fragmented, visibly eroding ruins of antiquity still lay haphazardly on the ground, evocative splinters of classical civilization. Brice took many photographs of landscape vistas and of the shards of ashlar masonry, fluted columns, molded entablatures and carved capitals, all jumbled together on the ground. He was aesthetically reenergized and redirected. In his own work, he had long been seeking to compare the individual's experience of life, both perceptual and emotional, with the grand scope of universal human experience. He now realized that this notion could be symbolized by reference to classical civilization." [5]

The ancient stone fragments that Brice saw contained their own primeval natural history, as naturally occurring material, as well as an indelible human history. William Brice describes: "the Greece I saw was not the Greece of the history books or the Greece of the museum treasures, it was Greece at my feet. It was a landscape of fragments, all in shambles, or in the process of reconstruction, shards, and memory, and remnants. Fragmented forms have long been present in my work, and there was something quite moving about all that was strewn upon the ground there. You pick up a rock, or is it a rock, it's a piece of something, a few indecipherable marks upon it, defaced and yet imbedded within it is the human presence." [6] Discovering a "human presence," "imbedded" in the stone—it is almost as if he were rediscovering a potent imaginative resource that he already understood and evinced in the early *Rock Formations*. But now it would manifest itself with new—and simultaneously ancient—imagery.

The emergence of Brice's mature "signature" style brought him to a new mode of abstraction that intersected his greater daring to present erotic subjects. The thighs, shoulders, breasts, hands, legs, back, stomach and buttocks were all there, as they had been in his more realistic renderings, together with newly prominent penile and vaginal forms, but he abstracted them like pictograms or hieroglyphs

5 —David Acton, "The Prints of William Brice," in William Brice: Works on Paper, 1982—1992.
(Los Angeles: Grunwald Center for the Graphic Arts, University of California, Los Angeles, 1993), p. 19.
6 — "Interview: Part I" by Wendy Diamond, Crown Point Press, San Francisco, December 1985;
reprinted in View, Vol. IV, No. 6, Spring 1988, p. 18, 20, Point Publications, San Francisco.

or talismans, as simplified as the features of stick figures. They were no longer the referents of the models whose bodies he drew and painted. Instead of belonging to his sitters, they now were the proprietary "stuff" of his own visual vocabulary and artistic imagination. Moreover, Brice allowed himself the privilege of putting these body parts together however he wished to suit his art and its visual poetics. Through his newfound abstraction, he was able to dissect the human body, putting it back together as a kind of visual collage of its parts without fidelity to true human form or anatomical structure. They did not have to add up to the appearance of a human form; it was enough—*powerfully* enough—to be evocatively and provocatively anthropomorphic.

Untitled (1973), a charcoal drawing, is a good example of his post-Greek style. The faintly human-like forms that float on the drawing's surface appear to be fragments of what may have been a stone carving of a female. The dominant central fragment appears

to be a pelvis and two thighs standing, almost ceremoniously, on a plinth. Hovering between this monumental fragment and the borders of the drawing paper are miscellaneous body parts: an (evident) arm and possibly some internal organs, but definitely biomorphic forms, all unattached, waiting to be restored in the viewer's imagination. Brice assigns the viewer not a passive role as a sensitive observer in this new style, but an active participating role as a wonderer, a conjurer, and maybe even

Untitled, 1973
compressed charcoal on paper
24 x 18 in. (61 x 45.7 cm)

a voyeur, in the way that spectators become voyeurs in looking at "hidden" photographs or medical illustrations—we do not merely see, we peer, we stare.

Untitled, 1984
oil on canvas, 108 x 108 in. (274.3 x 274.3 cm)
Collection of the Orange County Museum of Art

Over time, Brice's compositions became bolder and more complex, usually more emphatically sexual, and iconic in appearance. One such work is a grand, nine-foot-square untitled painting from 1984 in the collection of the Orange County Museum of Art. The canvas is visually bisected down the middle, setting up a left/right dialogue. On the left a vertical stack of rugged biomorphic masses painted in warm bluish grays reads as a distinctly masculine figure. Suggestions of phallic imagery—upright verticals, dual spheres— endow the figure with sexuality, even though the form is scarcely humanoid in shape. On the right, a similarly proportioned stack-up of forms is rendered much more

Untitled, 1998
oil on canvas, 103 x 143 in. (261.6 x 363.2 cm)
Collection of the Los Angeles County Museum of Art
Modern and Contemporary Art Acquisition Fund (AC1999.20.1)
Modern Art Department

diagrammatically, an outline of a figure limned in black lines over a warm grayish green background. Again, while not clearly depicting a human form, the figure is sexualized with vulvate and breast-like shapes. Both figures maintain equal visual claim on the viewer's imagination, and neither dominates the other. They exist, or co-exist, in a state of timeless equipoise.

But there is a third figure as well: in the upper part of the composition, straddling the empty space between this couple is a torso-like form that might almost be a schematic blueprint of a human being: shoulders, a spine, a pelvic bone are evident, as are squiggly shapes that may represent viscera. It is rendered as a pastiche of painted masses and black lines. Whether this third being is new life, or an interloping third party, or even a totemic emblem of sexual congress itself, is impossible to say. But the question, in addition to being unanswerable, does not ask to be answered; the power of this work, as with so many of Brice's paintings and drawings from the 1970s on, is its static, inscrutable mysteriousness. It is as if Brice had imbued it with a near-Olympian aloofness, not to be understood or adjudged, but to be recognized and to be undeniably present in the world, a fact of life.

As archetypal, Jungian, and psychologically compelling as his works from the 1970s and '80s were, by the 1990s, when the artist was now a septuagenarian,

Untitled,1998
oil on canvas, 108 ¹/₄ x 144 ¹/₄ in. (275 x 366.4 cm)
Collection of the Museum of Contemporary Art, Los Angeles
Purchased with funds provided by an anonymous donor (99.20)

they grew increasingly charged and primal. What had been erotic was now distilled, or amplified, to representations of an almost purely biological drive, literally a life force. His show of these late paintings, in 1998 at L.A. Louver, was dominated by about a dozen massive canvases painted for the exhibition. Their forms were strong and flat, brightly colored in a way reminiscent of the early American modernist Stuart Davis' paintings, but monumental in size and scale, visually bold and agitated at the same time. Describing the exhibition, critic Michael Duncan wrote that "sexual imagery abounds, often with lightning-bolt zigzags separating forms with masculine or feminine associations. In one work, a bright yellow lightning bolt vertically separates a lipstick-red, dress-like shape from an architectonic stack featuring two huge blue balls. The largest painting in the show presents a phallic piston shape immersed in a cavity made from two female torsos. In another of the large paintings, an upright rib cage and spinal column are juxtaposed with an egg-like womb. Set against a primary red background, these symbols together seem to engender a stack of burgeoning cells. Linking painting with procreation, Brice celebrates a sort of erotic biology." [7] Sexuality seems to have meant something more than ever for the aging Brice. In these late pictures, the echoes of the female nudes are still present, but they assert their presence not in erotic situations of longing, of apartness and reunion, but in the driving energy of living creatures.

The notion of a "trajectory" or "evolutionary arc" to describe an artist's aesthetic development is a fond conceit held by art historians, critics and curators who constitutionally attempt, as their professional responsibility, to discern an orderly narrative to account for individual artists and collective historical movements. This presumes—or at least desires—that an artist's development can be described as a progression of stages and phases, which culminates, finally, in a "breakthrough" mature or signature style. This commonplace schematic even allows for occasional fallow periods and epiphanies, recognizing that artistic genius is, after all, a human attribute and prone to the same distractions of attention and motivation that "ordinary" people must cope with.

But rarely does any artist's day-to-day studio practice and eventual development yield a template as clear and "parse-able" and uni-directional as the idea of a clear trajectory implies. For William Brice, the day-to-day creative life was largely worked out in the activity of drawing. "Drawing," William Brice said, "is a continuous activity for me. Increasingly I find that I want to act upon any idea or image that passes through my mind. I want to grasp it, to mark it. I also find that one drawing begets another, and the

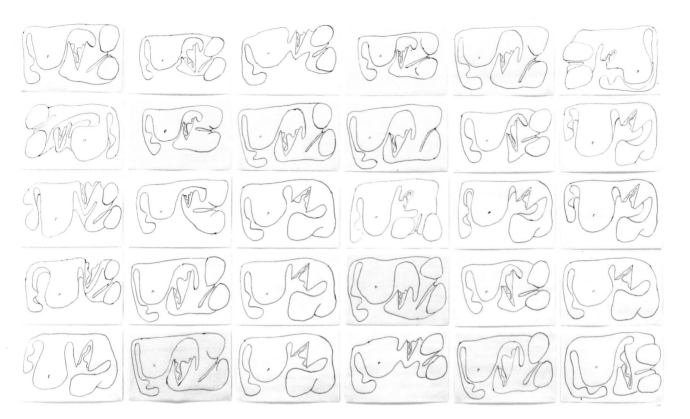

Untitled (Suite of 30 small drawings), 1991
ballpoint pen drawings on board
24 ¼ x 40 in. (61.6 x 101.6 cm)

idea develops. I rarely use a drawing as a direct study for a painting. The drawings have
a life of their own. They establish a vocabulary that I develop in painting. So the
drawings and the paintings coexist.... It's significant that some of the most moving works
are achieved in drawing." [8] Thus to know Brice's art it is essential, perhaps more than it
is for most other artists known primarily as painters, to regard the drawings, collectively,
as a major arena of activity, not as a sidelight to his paintings, but as a crucible for his
daily creativity and artistic self-awareness. The drawings in the present exhibition span
much of Brice's career, and constitute a core sample of his life in the studio from the late
1950s through the mid-1980s. In one mode or another, the female nude is the dominant

7 —Michael Duncan, "William Brice at L.A. Louver," in Art in America, February 1999, p. 118
8 —"Interview: Part I" by Wendy Diamond, Crown Point Press, San Francisco, December 1985;
reprinted in View, Vol. IV, No. 6, Spring 1988, p. 2, Point Publications, San Francisco.

subject throughout, increasingly abstract and increasingly sexualized, but always birthed by the womanly form, the female figure. What does it mean to have hewed with a career-long fidelity to the figurative tradition—especially, starting at a time when abstract gestural painting was supremely ascendant? As Richard Armstrong commented in his exceptionally thoughtful catalogue essay for the 1986 paintings and drawings survey organized by Los Angeles' Museum of Contemporary Art and sponsored by the Fellows of Contemporary Art, "A gregarious man by nature, Brice is a loner as an artist. Though he joined the art faculty at the University of California, Los Angeles in 1953, quickly becoming one of its most popular and respected members, the 1950s remained a period of relative isolation for him as he pursued an out of fashion, solitary aesthetic based on direct observation of nature." [9] It is safe to say that the same isolation prevailed after abstract expressionism was succeeded in turn by pop art, minimalism, conceptual art and all the other artistic advents in the international free-for-all that constitutes contemporary art in the 21st century, all of which Brice observed directly.

Woman and Land, 1956
charcoal and sanguine chalk on paperboard
40 1/16 x 32 in. (101.1 x 81.3 cm)
Collection of the Hirshhorn Museum and Sculpture Garden
Gift of Joseph H. Hirshhorn, 1966,
Accession Number: 66.617

Figuration, venerable as it always was and will be, must have seemed to many to be anything but avant-garde—indeed archaic—when Brice embarked down that road; and Brice's beloved classicism must have impressed some as being not merely anachronistic but positively archaeological. Surely, his fidelity was not merely to an out-of-date mode as it was to his principles and personal aesthetic. But, rather than being a simple holdout for the values or the past, or a committed contrarian to the present, he might be well understood as a forerunner of a later, soon-to-be-described-as "post-Modern" sensibility—an activist in the name of artistic independence, not so much from the past as from the hegemony of current practice. Though he experimented, he resisted the dictates and the shibboleths of the present. Brice, who had a demonstrably sophisticated understanding of abstract expressionism and later currents of art practice, plainly did not want to be dragooned by prevailing artistic ideology as he developed his own ideas. Brice most assuredly did not absent himself from art history, past or present; he engaged it. Far from holding out against something, he was staking out to embrace something quite different and independent. His stance was a kind of precursor or a presage of what would later come to characterize the determined independence of most artists working today. But in pursuit of his intensely personal vision, and impelled by deep-rooted psychological realities that haunted his inner life, he worked in professional solitude to create an autographic body of work.

It is not just an artist's inner spirit that may inspire and shape creativity; spirit of place may sharply inflect it as well. John Brice has often remarked on his father's love of California; and in William Brice's pre-Greek art, the landscape elements that appear frequently are images inspired by the Southern California land, from the stones and rocks to the sea to the foliage and the trees—especially the eucalyptus trees that still thrive just outside his home. Clearly, Brice was artistically influenced by and felt aesthetically "at home" in Los Angeles. But it is worth speculating on his professional choice early on to stake his artistic career in Los Angeles, at such a remove from New York, the perceived epicenter of the international art world at the time. Had he gone to

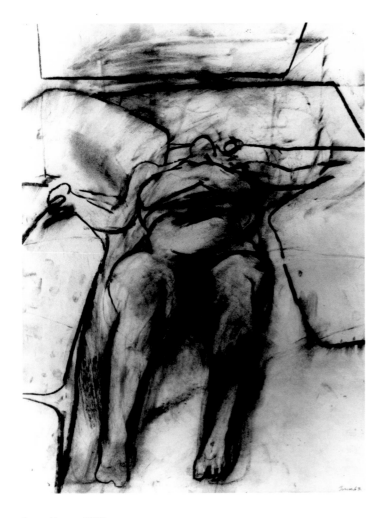

Large Figure, 1963
charcoal on paper, sheet: 25 x 18 in. (63.5 x 45.7 cm).
Collection of the Whitney Museum of American Art
Purchase 65.38

New York in the 1950s, as was *de rigueur* for so many aspiring young artists, it is probable—likely, in fact—that following his early incursion into abstract painting, Brice would have been encouraged by peers, dealers, collectors and interested critics to do more of it and with it—to develop his engagement with abstraction all the more. And, had he become an abstractionist in New York and subsequently attempted to return to representational figuration, as he did do in Los Angeles, it is just as likely that he'd have been derided as atavistic and retrogressive by those who earlier would have applauded his abstraction. He'd probably have gotten kicked around until it hurt sorely; or so we can speculate. In any case, Brice, for reasons we cannot know—and which perhaps he himself did not know—chose not to make art in New York.

Los Angeles artists at that same time did not benefit from a highly developed art critical milieu, nor did they suffer from the hyperventilation of art ideologues.

A pronounced critical latitude pervaded the Los Angeles art scene during that period, and far from being factionalized and fractious, the artistic community—as has been noted in many accounts by contemporaneous artists, observers and art historians—it was animated by a spirit of open-minded interest and mutual supportiveness among its denizens. While there were some incipient artistic directions taking hold among Southern California artists—variously described as the "Beat Generation" (Ed Kienholz, Wallace Berman, George Herms), the "Light-and-Space" artists (Robert Irwin, James Turrell, Larry Bell), and figures pioneering in a distinctively narrative art form that did not yet go by the name of "Conceptual Art" (John Baldessari, Ed Ruscha, Eleanor Antin)—they peaceably coexisted in the wide-open creative space of the SoCal art world of the day.

In this milieu, a welcoming, nondoctrinaire embrace of individual visions flourished. Brice's choice to remain in the burgeoning, laid-back, artistically libertine artistic community of Los Angeles proved fortuitous, providing a supportive environment that nurtured his inner nature and enabled this complex, jovial and private soul to develop his idiomatic art in its varying forms. Brice explored numerous stylistic shifts through his artistic development. A rhythm of artistic wanderlust united with an abidance by figuration, eroticism and sexuality defined his art throughout. Doing what he did—working in quiet isolation in his studio—where he did—in the gregarious, supportive intellectual climate of the emergent Los Angeles art world—enabled him to thrive as "an artist's artist."

Howard N. Fox *is curator emeritus of contemporary art,*
Los Angeles County Museum of Art.

DRAWINGS
1960–1985

Untitled
charcoal on paper
16 ³/₄ x 21 ¹/₂ in. (42.5 x 54.6 cm)

1961

Untitled
charcoal on paper
25 x 19 in. (63.5 x 48.3 cm)

1961

Reclining Figure
charcoal on paper
26 1/4 x 19 1/4 in. (66.7 x 48.9 cm)

Untitled
charcoal on paper
19 x 25 $^1/_4$ in. (48.3 x 64.1 cm)

Untitled
charcoal on paper
25 x 19 in. (63.5 x 48.3 cm)

c. 1964

Untitled
charcoal on paper
19 x 24 in. (48.3 x 61 cm)

Untitled
charcoal on paper
24 x 18 in. (61 x 45.7 cm)

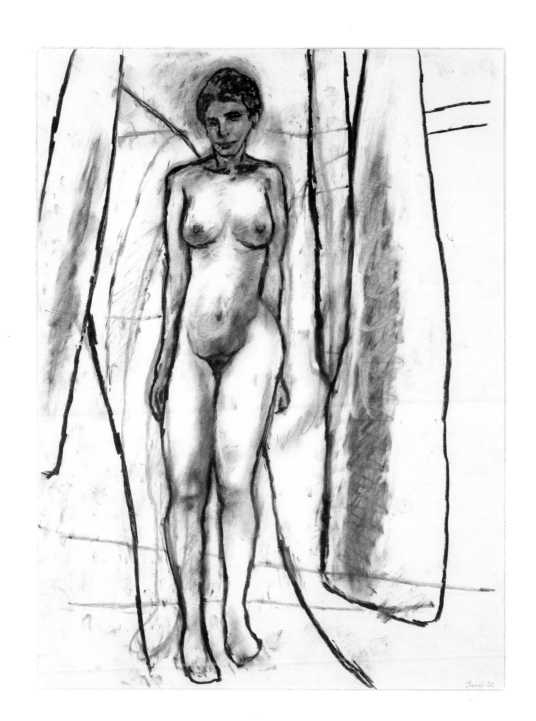

1965

Untitled
graphite on tracing paper
24 x 19 in. (61 x 48.3 cm)

1965

Untitled
charcoal on paper
24 x 19 in. (61 x 48.3 cm)

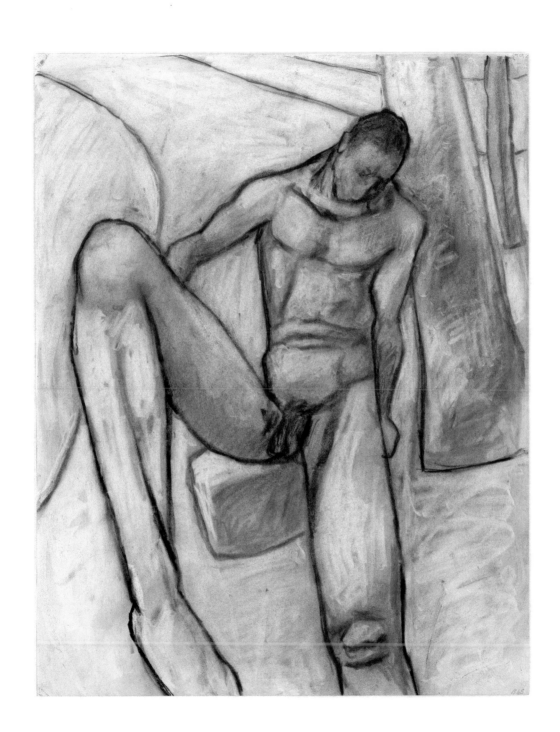

1967

Untitled
charcoal on paper
24 x 19 in. (61 x 48.3 cm)

Reclining Figure with Blue and Green Pond
pastel on paper
23 ³/₄ x 18 ³/₄ in. (60.3 x 47.6 cm)

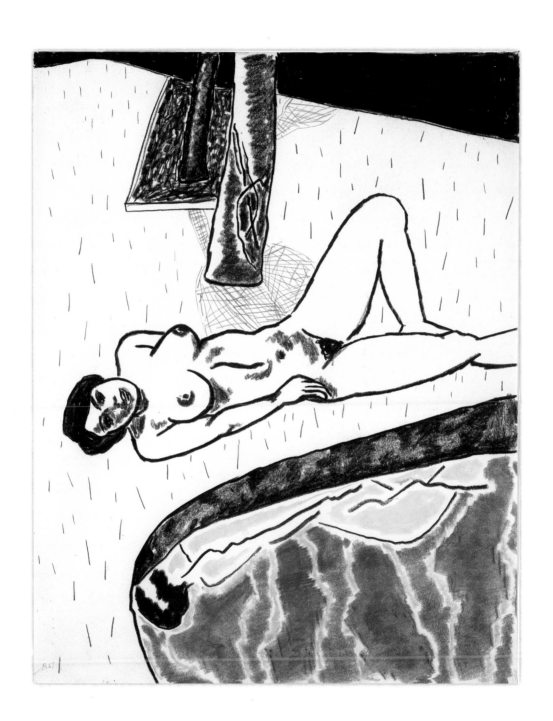

B.67

1967

Untitled
pastel on paper
25 x 19 in. (63.5 x 48.3 cm)

Untitled
ink pen on paper
24 x 18 ⁷/₈ in. (61 x 47.9 cm)

Untitled
charcoal on paper
24 x 18 in. (61 x 45.7 cm)

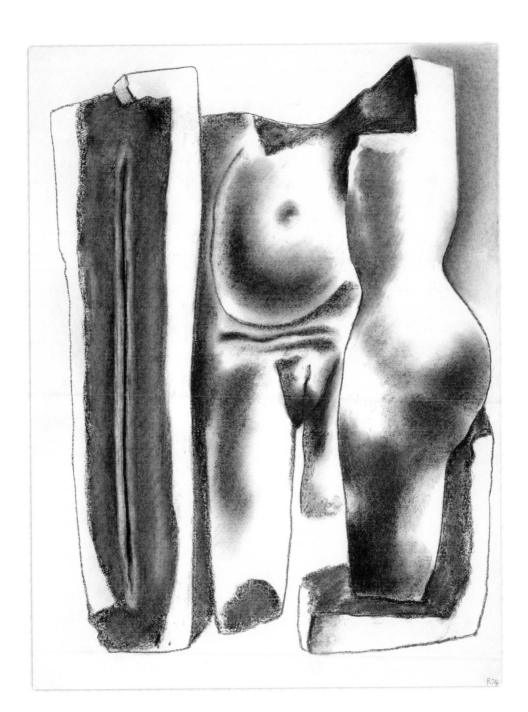

B.74

c. 1977

Untitled
charcoal on paper
18 x 24 in. (45.7 x 61 cm)

1977

Untitled
oil pastel on paper
19 x 24 $^1/_2$ in. (48.3 x 62.2 cm)

Untitled
ink on paper
23 ³/₄ x 17 ⁷/₈ in. (60.3 x 45.4 cm)

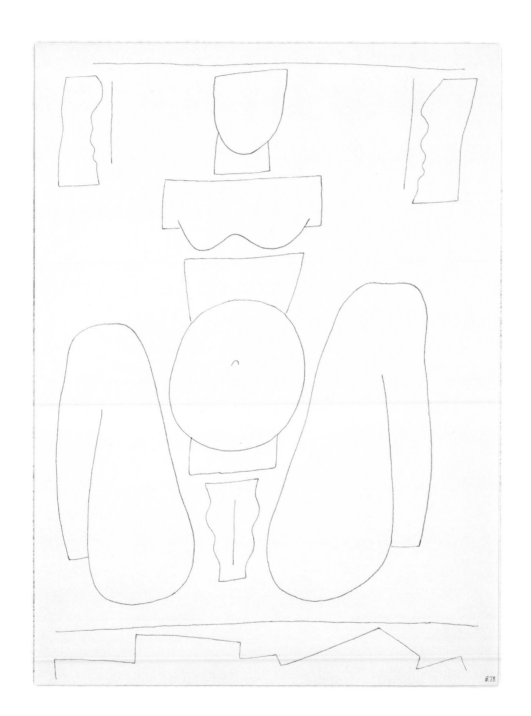

6.78

Untitled
charcoal on paper
24 x 18 in. (61 x 45.7 cm)

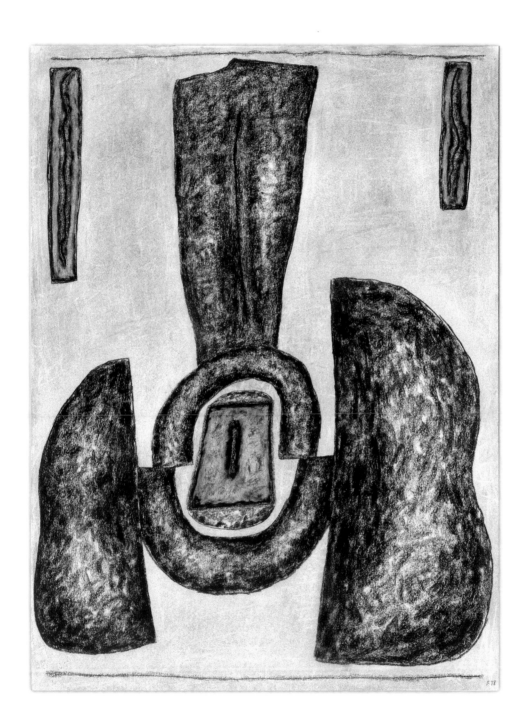

Untitled
charcoal on paper
24 x 18 in. (61 x 45.7 cm)

1980

Untitled
ink on paper
17 ⁷/₈ x 23 ³/₄ in. (45.4 x 60.3 cm)

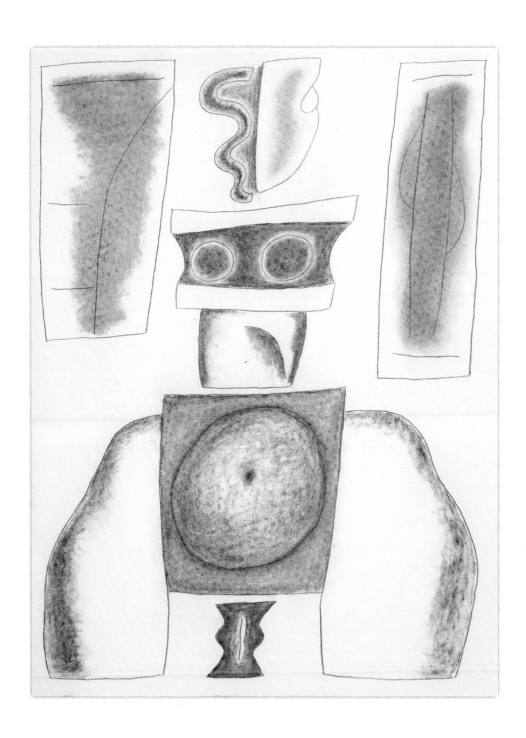

c. 1980

Untitled
ink pen on paper
24 x 18 in. (61 x 45.7 cm)

Untitled
ink drawing on paper
17 7/8 x 23 3/4 in. (45.4 x 60.3 cm)

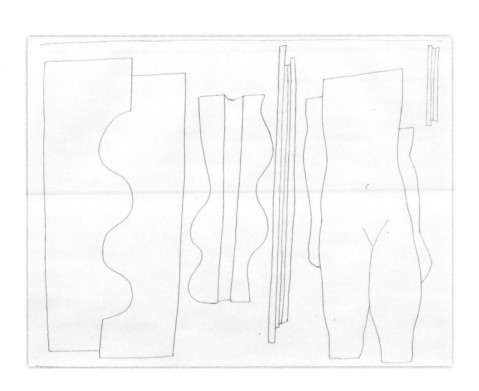

c. 1980

Untitled
charcoal on paper
24 x 18 in. (61 x 45.7 cm)

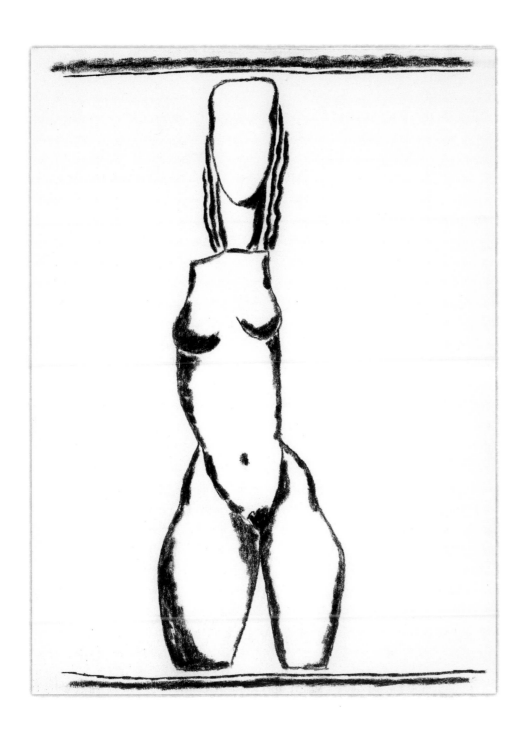

c. 1980

Untitled
charcoal on paper
18 x 24 in. (45.7 x 61 cm)

Untitled
pastel and graphite on paper
24 x 17 3/4 in. (61 x 45.1 cm)

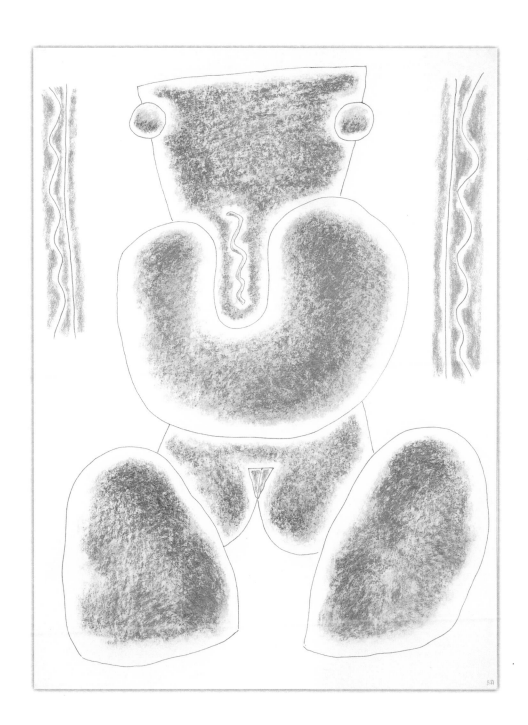

Untitled
ink pen and charcoal on paper
24 x 18 in. (61 x 45.7 cm)

B.81

Untitled
ink on paper
24 x 18 in. (61 x 45.7 cm)

Untitled
charcoal and ink pen on paper
24 x 18 in. (61 x 45.7 cm)

c. 1981

Untitled
pastel and ink on paper
24 x 18 in. (61 x 45.7 cm)

Untitled
charcoal on paper
24 x 18 in. (61 x 45.7 cm)

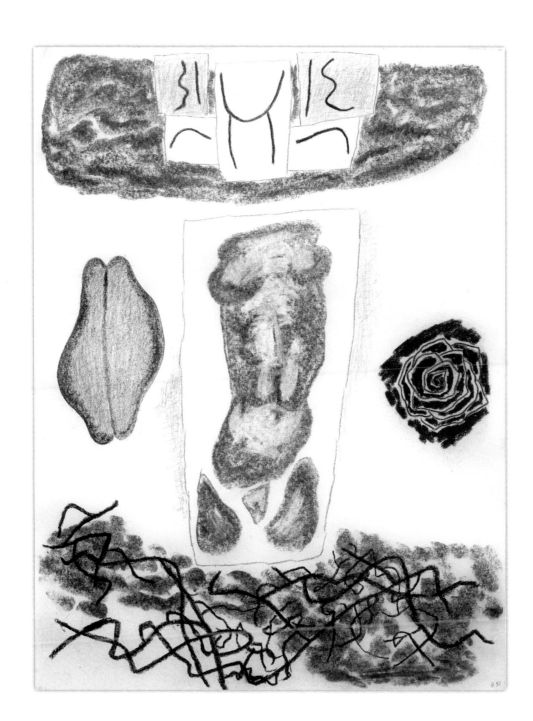

Untitled
charcoal and pastel on paper
24 x 18 in. (61 x 45.7 cm)

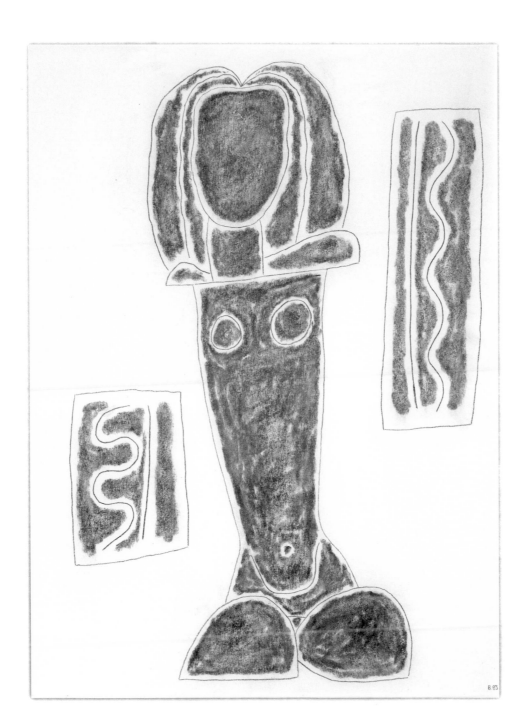

Untitled
pastel and charcoal on paper
24 x 18 in. (61 x 45.7 cm)

Untitled
charcoal and ink on paper
24 x 18 in. (61 x 45.7 cm)

B.84

c. 1984

Untitled
pastel and ink pen on paper
18 x 24 in. (45.7 x 61 cm)

1985

Untitled
ink on paper
24 x 18 in. (61 x 45.7 cm)

CHRONOLOGY

CHRONOLOGY

clockwise from top: Fanny Brice;
Jules "Nicky" Arnstein;
Arnstein and James Cagney;
Frances, Fanny and William Brice;
Frances and William

1921 William Jules Brice was born on April 23, in New York City, the second child of the Broadway star Fanny Brice and Jules "Nicky" Arnstein — his sister Frances was born in 1919. His mother was a tough, driven perfectionist, while his father was a gambler and con artist with extravagant tastes. Nicky was essentially absent, first incarcerated for securities fraud when Brice was an infant, then estranged after he and Fanny divorced in 1927. The demands of stardom kept Fanny late at the theater and on the road touring, leaving Brice and his sister largely to the charge of French governesses, who looked after the children in the Brices' luxurious brown stone in New York's East Side, and on summer holidays in Europe.

1929 Still living in New York City, his mother married Billy Rose in a ceremony officiated by Mayor James Walker in New York. They had met much earlier, when he was a stenographic clerk to her friend, financier and presidential advisor Bernard Baruch.

Rose had become an extremely successful lyricist and Broadway producer, and the Brice household was constantly filled with lively personalities, revered intellects and accomplished artists, including the likes of George and Ira Gershwin, Will Rogers, Clifford Odets, John Barrymore, Katherine Hepburn, Averell Harriman and Edward, Prince of Wales.

Fanny's general interest in art influenced her son, who was exposed at an early age to Old Masters and modern art, on visits to New York museums and travels in Europe.

1933 Brice began to show a keen interest in and talent for art, and Fanny encouraged her son by engaging artist Henry Botkin (a first cousin to the Gershwins) as his tutor. In addition to lessons and museum visits, Botkin took Brice to galleries where he saw art of that time, contemporary in 1933, and was introduced to many of the artists who were friends of Botkin's and part of the New York art scene.

top: William Brice as a boy
middle and bottom: Fanny Brice and Billy Rose

1934 Brice bought his first work of art, a gouache by Pablo Picasso entitled *Child in Drawers*, 1906, with money he was given by his mother in lieu of a bar mitzvah.

1938 Following her divorce from Rose, Fanny moved with Brice and his sister to Beverly Hills, and began her radio career. Fanny again collected an engaging circle of friends, professionals in radio and film, many of whom were building art collections that included new, modern pieces.

Brice enrolled in Cumnock School for Expression, an experimental, arts-focused junior college in Los Angeles. It was there where he met and dated Shirley Bardeen, whom he later married.

1939–40 Brice returned to New York City and lived with Henry Botkin and his family, while he attended Art Students League. An atelier school with a modern emphasis, Brice developed

his skills in drawing and painting in its innovative environment. Brice's relationship to Botkin was formative, and he claimed he not only learned about art from Botkin, but most importantly about the life of an artist. In response to Botkin's passing in 1983, Brice wrote:

Opposite page
top: Pablo Picasso, *Child in Drawers (Enfant au Caleçon)*
1906, gouache on paper
24 ¹/₂ x 16 ¹/₂ in. (62.2 x 41.9 cm)
Courtesy of the Estate of William Brice
middle: "Domestic" scenes in Fanny Brice's home
bottom: Postcard depicting Fanny Brice's estate

This page
left: Henry Botkin in his studio
right: Botkin and Brice

"Harry, so long now dear to me... opened to me a view of passionate engagement in the practice of art. Tough minded and discerning, he was enthusiastically appreciative, capable of being deeply moved by the wonder of it—art. He was totally absorbed in it and conveyed to me through his gentle teaching and infinite patience and through his own creative process a value in life commitment. In his subtle and resolute persistence, his integrity of conviction and sensibility he was confident of his own powers as an artist but remained ceaselessly open and questioning, never complacent and never arrogant..."

1939
Brice's sister Frances married Ray Stark, an extremely energetic and quick-minded man, who became one of Hollywood's legendary agents and producers. Brice's and Stark's relationship would transcend that of brothers-in-law, and the men became fast friends. Eventually, Stark engaged Brice as the Starks' art consultant, assisting them to amass an important collection of 19th and 20th century painting and sculpture at their Holmby Hills home, and later at the Stark Ranch just north of Santa Barbara, in the Santa Ynez Valley.

1940–42
Back in Los Angeles, Brice finished high school and enrolled in Chouinard Art Institute, while also taking occasional classes at other schools, including Otis Art Institute. At Otis, he met two artists in particular with whom he developed long friendships and professional relationships — Howard Warshaw and Rico LeBrun.

1942

Brice briefly worked for Metro-Goldwyn-Mayer Studios, designing sets and painting "masterpieces" for their films, creating ersatz Cézannes and Rembrandts.

Brice married Shirley Bardeen on August 23 in Las Vegas. The couple was driven there by Fanny and her then-boyfriend, actor John Conte.

On October 12, Brice enlisted in the Army Air Corps. One of his responsibilities was to paint murals in officers' mess halls at military installations in the western United States.

Opposite page
top: Brice, Bardeen, Warshaw
and friends in costume
middle: Brice, Rico LeBrun
and Howard Warshaw
bottom: Brice in his studio, 1940s

This page
top: The Brices on vacation
in Mexico, 1940s
bottom: Shirley and William Brice

1943 Brice received a medical discharge from the Army due to asthma, and Brice and his wife returned to Los Angeles. They moved into Fanny's pool house, where they lived for seven years, in order to give Brice the opportunity to pursue painting.

1947 Brice paintings were included in two important national group exhibitions. In *The 8th Annual Exhibition of Artists of Los Angeles and Vicinity* at the Los Angeles County Museum, he won second prize for painting. The show received press coverage in the Los Angeles Times and Los Angeles Herald-Express, although it was a controversial exhibition to the public. In October, Brice's submission was accepted to the annual exhibition, *Painting in the United States, 1947*, at Carnegie Institute in Pittsburgh, Pennsylvania. Initiated in 1943, this annual exhibition was the predecessor of the prestigious Carnegie International.

Opposite page
Fanny Brice, Frances Brice,
and William and Shirley Brice at home

This page
top: Brice in his studio, late 1940s
bottom: Studio image of *Rock Composition I*, 1947,
oil on canvas, 7 x 18 in. (17.8 x 45.7 cm)

His first one-person exhibition *Paintings by William Brice, Los Angeles* opened on November 16 at the Santa Barbara Museum of Art. The show received lengthy and glowing reviews in the Santa Barbara News-Press.

1948 Brice was invited to teach at Jepson Art Institute, Los Angeles, by Herbert Jepson, where his friends Howard Warshaw and Rico LeBrun also taught. The school, founded by Jepson in 1945, closed in 1954.

1949 Brice had his first one-man exhibition in a commercial venue, at Downtown Gallery in New York City, from February 15 to March 5.

1950 Brice's only child, John, was born in Los Angeles.

Brice purchased architect Richard Neutra's avant-garde "Plywood House," which was built in 1936 as a show house. Originally "exhibited" on Los Angeles' Miracle Mile, the building was relocated to Brentwood before Brice purchased it. Brice immediately added a studio constructed by a Neutra associate; although approximate to his home, it was not a place where others were welcome. The home became a hub for the Brices' vibrant social life, while Brice considered his studio a private space.

Opposite page
top: The Brices and the Warshaws
middle: Shirley Brice, pregnant with son John
bottom: Brice outside of his home

This page
top: Brice in the Santa Monica Mountains
bottom: The "Plywood House,"
designed by Richard Neutra

Brice had his first Los Angeles area one-man show in a commercial venue, *New Watercolors by William Brice,* at Frank Perls Gallery, Beverly Hills, from April 20 to May 16. Perls, who opened his gallery in 1939, showed young L.A. talent alongside important European modernists, and was central to building many prominent collections in Los Angeles. Brice continued to show with Frank Perls Gallery through the 1960s.

The Brices became extremely close with Perls and his wife Ann, remaining so until Perls' death in 1975.

1951

On May 30, Fanny died of a cerebral hemorrhage. For the first time, Brice was without the larger-than-life presence of his mother.

Brice worked with Lynton R. Kistler, the only master printer of lithography in Los Angeles at that time, to produce his first print, *Three Heads.*

top to bottom: Frank Perls; Brice in his studio;
Three Heads, 1951, lithograph, 18 x 22 7/8 in. (45.7 x 58 cm),
edition of 25, printed by Lynton Kistler

1954 Brice left Jepson Art Institute to accept a position as acting assistant professor at the University of California, Los Angeles.

1955 One-man exhibitions at Frank Perls Gallery in Beverly Hills and The Alan Gallery in New York City garnered positive press and sales for Brice.

1957 Brice was promoted to assistant professor at UCLA, his first step up the university's academic ladder. He was promoted to associate professor in 1958, to professor in 1965, and awarded Professor Emeritus status in 1991, after 38 years.

Joseph Hirshhorn purchased three drawings from The Alan Gallery, New York City. Hirshhorn eventually acquired 70 works on paper that are now in the collection of the Smithsonian's Hirshhorn Museum and Sculpture Garden in Washington, D.C.

top to bottom: Art Building (now Perloff Hall), UCLA, c. 1952; drawing by Brice of Perls; Joe Hirshhorn and Brice at Frank Perls Gallery

Brice experimented with intaglio, helped in the process by UCLA colleague John Paul Jones, who taught printmaking.

1958   Brice was granted a six-month sabbatical from UCLA for a research project in Europe to study fresco painting. Traveling by car, the Brice family stopped at museums and churches as they crisscrossed France, Italy and Switzerland. Although he had been to Europe in his youth and had seen his share of museums there and in New York, Brice used this opportunity to immerse himself in the art and architecture of those countries without distraction.

1961   Awarded a Ford Foundation Grant for work with Tamarind Lithography Workshop in Los Angeles (established in 1960), Brice produced 24 prints between November 24 and April 25, 1962. Founded by June Wayne, Tamarind helped revitalize printmaking in the US.

Brice was featured in *Time Magazine,* his first recognition by a national publication, in an article reviewing his exhibition at The Alan Gallery, New York City.

1962   Brice traveled with close friends to Mexico, visiting Aztec ruins and calling on Rufino Tamayo. The prominent Mexican artist had met Brice earlier on a visit to Los Angeles, triggered by the fact that Fanny owned and bequeathed to William a large Tamayo painting. The strong shapes and forms of both the ancient architecture and 20th century Mexican murals made a strong impression on Brice.

Opposite page
top to bottom: The Brices in Italy,
and with Frank Perls in Venice, 1958;
Woman in a Flowered Blouse, 1962, lithograph,
30 x 22 1/4 in. (76.2 x 56.5 cm), edition of 20,
published by Tamarind Workshop, Los Angeles

This page
top: At the home of Rufino Tamayo, Mexico, 1962
bottom: Brice working in Tamarind
Lithography Workshop

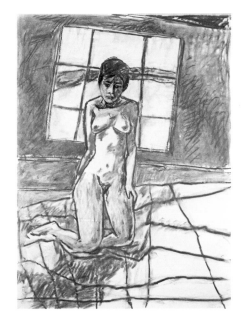

top: Kneeling Figure And Window, 1964
charcoal on paper, 23 7/8 x 18 in. (60.7 x 45.7 cm)
Collection of the Hirshhorn Museum and Sculpture Garden
Gift of Joseph H. Hirshhorn, 1966; Accession Number: 66.640
bottom: Interior IV, 1963, oil and magna on canvas,
56 x 68 in. (142.2 x 172.7 cm)

As he continued work with Tamarind Institute, he developed a series of prints that included the appearance of color for the first time. Brice used only black ink in all his preceding prints.

1964 *Funny Girl,* a musical based on the life of Fanny and Nicky, opened on Broadway. Both the musical and 1968 film starring Barbra Streisand were produced by Ray Stark; neither mention Fanny having children to keep the story simple. *Funny Girl* brought renewed fame and a new generation of fans to Fanny.

1966 Good friend and fellow artist Richard Diebenkorn joined the faculty at UCLA, and taught there until 1973. The two men and their wives were extremely close until Diebenkorn's death in 1993.

Brice was again invited by Tamarind Institute for a third lithography session.

1968 Brice was granted a second sabbatical from UCLA. He moved his family into a flat in London's Chelsea, where he also rented

a studio. He hoped the break from Los Angeles would allow him to discover the new direction in his work he sought, as well as enjoy time with friends and fellow artists David Hockney and R.B. Kitaj, in particular. He was also introduced to others, such as Henry Moore.

Near the end of his stay in London, Brice encountered "Herostratus," a 1967 experimental feature by Don Levy. Its mosaic of staccato iconography pushed emotional and conceptual buttons in the artist. The film was a pivotal influence—Brice began to experiment with conceptualized content that juxtaposed fragments and motifs, and contemporary pictorial references.

1970 Brice sailed with family and friends through the Greek islands. Captivated by the light and stone ruins, Brice derived from this ancient landscape a more personal and timeless iconography. Along with his discoveries two years prior, this moment defined a turning point in his development; fragments of antiquities began to loom large in the content of his paintings, drawings and prints.

top: Fragments, 1968, oil on canvas, 28 x 28 in. (71.1 x 71.1 cm)
middle: The Brices in Greece, 1970
bottom: Untitled, 1978, oil on canvas, 92 x 68 in. (233.7 x 172.7 cm)

1970–75
Brice immersed himself in studio work, and declined to exhibit while focused on the developing vocabulary of iconography and imagery inspired by London and Greece.

1975
Brice moved from the studio adjacent to his home to an industrial space in Santa Monica. The skylights and large expanse allowed Brice to explore a different scale and sense of light to his painting.

1978
Works from 1970–1975 were shown in associated exhibitions at the Los Angeles Institute of Contemporary Art (LAICA), and Nicholas Wilder Gallery, also in Los Angeles.

top: Brice in his studio, 1980
bottom: *Untitled*, 1980, oil on canvas,
102 x 90 in. (259 x 228.6 cm)

1979 Brice revisited Greece to further investigate the sources of his inspiration and vocabulary.

Brice illustrated the publication of friend and fellow UCLA faculty member Jascha Kessler, entitled *Bearing Gifts*.

1980 Brice had his first solo exhibition with Robert Miller Gallery in New York.

1984 Brice again moved studios, this time to a warehouse in the San Fernando Valley, an area away from other artists or art venues.

Brice had his first exhibition at L.A. Louver in Venice, California—his first of four solo shows with the gallery.

top: David Hockney, *Bill Brice, Santa Monica, June 1970*, color photograph, 4 x 6 in. (10.2 x 15.2 cm), Copyright David Hockney
middle: Untitled, 1984, oil on canvas, 21 1/8 x 27 1/4 in. (53.7 x 69.2 cm)
bottom: Brice, David Hockney and Richard Diebenkorn at Brice's exhibition opening, L.A. Louver, 1984

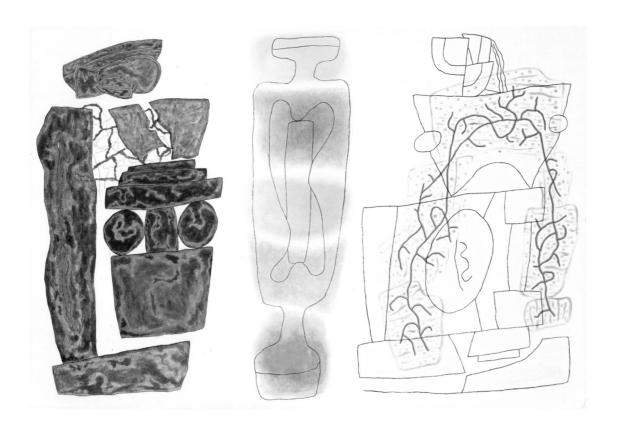

This page
top: *Untitled #5 (Ivory Field)*, 1985, color aquatint
with soft ground and hard ground etching and spit bite
aquatint, 29 ³/₄ x 44 in. (68 x 111.8 cm), edition of 25,
published by Crown Point Press, San Francisco
bottom: Brice with printer Hidekatsu Takada in the
Crown Point Press studio, 1985

Opposite page
Installation photography of Brice's retrospective
exhibition at the Museum of Contemporary Art, 1986

1985

Brice was invited to work at Crown Point Press in San Francisco with press owner and master printer Kathan Brown. He created a series of intaglio prints, the first in this medium in more than 20 years. This collaboration produced an extremely successful group of six prints, fully exploiting Brice's iconography and palette. In a 1985 interview at Crown Point Press, he said, *"Sense of scale does not depend on the proportional relationship of forms. It also has to do with the way the surface is experienced. One of the determinants of scale is time. How long it takes to get from one place to another... I think my elaboration of surface has to do with a quality of time."*

Brice illustrated another of Jascha Kessler's publications, *Transmigrations*.

1986 *William Brice: A Selection of Painting and Drawing, 1947–1986* was mounted by the Museum of Contemporary Art at the Temporary Contemporary in Los Angeles, and was the first major retrospective of the artist's work. The exhibition, curated by Julia Brown Turrell with Ann Goldstein as project director, included 49 paintings and 25 works on paper. This survey exhibition later traveled to the Grey Art Gallery and Study Center at New York University.

Brice participated in Crown Point Press' Japanese woodblock print program, collaboratively creating a piece in the *ukiyo-e* tradition using inks with a different composition than those used in lithography and intaglio printing. The experience of working with Crown Point Press inspired him to increase his use of watercolor.

1988
Brice received a Ford Foundation Grant for an experimental collaborative printmaking project with Robert Aull, a master intaglio printer in Los Angeles.

1989
Brice had his second exhibition at L.A. Louver, with new drawings.

1990
Notations 1982 was organized by Los Angeles County Museum of Art (April 5– May 27). The exhibition included 48 drawings made on 4" x 6" file cards that Brice would always have with him, in or away from the studio, and about which Brice said *"Drawing is a continuous activity for me."*

Brice worked on lithography with Tamarind Institute, which had moved to Albuquerque and become a part of University of New Mexico. He also revisited Crown Point Press in San Francisco to experiment with aquatint resulting another evocative series of prints.

Ann Rosener (Perls), who had been on the 1979 visit to Greece, invited Brice to collaborate in the production of a livre d'artiste called *In Simple Clothes*. The etchings he produced with Robert Aull accompanied newly translated writings of Greek poet Constantine P. Cavafy (1863– 1933). *In Simple Clothes* was a two-year project published by Rosener's letterpress Occasional Works, in Woodside, California, and was released in 1992.

Brice had his third solo exhibition at L.A. Louver, this time of watercolor paintings.

1991

Brice retired from UCLA after a 38-year association, and began to spend an increasing amount of time alone in his studio, which continued to be a private place where others were seldom invited.

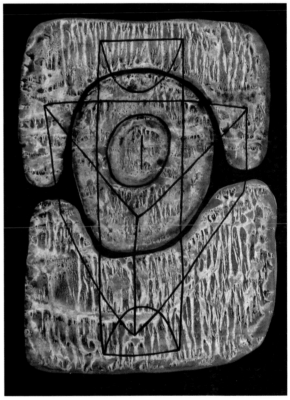

Opposite page
top: The Brices and the Diebenkorns at the Stark Ranch in Los Olivos, California, 1986
middle: Shirley Brice, Fran Stark, William Brice and Ray Stark
bottom: Brice and Diebenkorn in Japan, 1987;
Kyoto, 1987, color woodcut, 41 x 28 in. (104 x 71.1 cm), edition of 100, published by Crown Point Press, San Francisco

This page
top: Installation photography of *William Brice: Watercolors* at L.A. Louver, 1990
bottom: Untitled #1, 1990, watercolor on paper, 24 x 18 in. (61 x 45.7 cm)

1992

Brice's sister, Frances Stark, died on May 31.

1993

William Brice: Works on Paper 1982–1992 at UCLA's Grunwald Center for the Graphic Arts honored the recently retired Brice. The exhibition of prints and drawings also included a catalogue raisonné of his editioned works.

1998

Brice had his final solo exhibition, of new paintings, at L.A. Louver. All of the works in the show were placed into important private and institutional collections, including the Los Angeles County Museum of Art and the Museum of Contemporary Art, Los Angeles. The show received great critical attention, garnering reviews in *Art in America*, *LA Weekly* and the *Los Angeles Times*.

top: Christmas at the Stark residence, 1990. {Front row, left to right: Allison Gorsuch (Stark), daughter of Wendy Stark, granddaughter of Fran and Ray Stark; Fran Stark (William Brice's sister); Sandra Saxon (Brice) with Saxon Brice on her lap; Francis Brody; Edna Mchugh (daughter of Eddie Cantor). Back row, left to right: William Brice, Shirley Brice, John Brice, Margaret Booth (film editor); John Morrissey (Wendy Stark's husband); Wendy Stark; Ray Stark.}
bottom: Cover of *William Brice: Works on Paper*, published by the Grunwald Center for the Graphic Arts, 1993

*"Brice—an unquestioned virtuoso—set
himself a difficult challenge. All paintings
appear to consciously run the risk of being
boring. All are composed of two-dimensional
shapes largely self-contained. They take
no obvious advantage of standard devices
for achieving illusionistic volume, deep
space or interlocking drama. Formal
elements tend to be isolated and self-
absorbed. In a lesser artist, this would be
a prescription for failure. But Brice uses
less to bring off more.*

*Speaking of the old less-is-more cliché,
the artist actually revised the tack
of reductivist art to remind us that
painting can still be something more
than pure phenomenon or mere formality.
The net effect of his astringent cocktail
of sensibilities makes a place where the lyric
meets the epic, energy confronts exhaustion,
and rapture boogies with anxiety."*

William Wilson, *Los Angeles Times,*
November 16, 1998

Installation photography of Brice's exhibition at L.A. Louver, 1998

top: Stark Mock-Walk of Garden Terrace with Brice at the Getty Center, September 2005
middle: The Ray and Fran Stark Sculpture Terrace
bottom: The Ray and Fran Stark Sculpture Garden

2004   Ray Stark died on January 17. With his passing, the majority of the Starks' formidable collection of sculpture was donated to the J. Paul Getty Museum. Twenty-eight pieces of modern and contemporary sculpture were designated to be installed on the grounds of the Getty Center as The Fran and Ray Stark Sculpture Collection, including works by Alexander Calder, Mark di Suvero, Elizabeth Frink, Alberto Giacometti, Ellsworth Kelly, Aristide Maillol, Henry Moore, Isamu Noguchi, George Rickey, Joel Shapiro, Peter Shelton and William Turnbull.

2007   As advisor to the The Fran And Ray Stark Foundation, Brice worked with Antonia Bostrom and Christopher Bedford, curator and consulting curator of sculpture and decorative arts, Merritt Price, Getty Exhibition Design Manager, and many others, to install The Fran and Ray Stark Sculpture Collection at the Getty Center.

Brice's grandson and John's son, Saxon Brice, worked in the studio during the summer.

2008 Brice fell while
out shopping
in preparation for a dinner to be shared
with good friends, and died without
regaining consciousness on March 3.

Untitled, 2007
oil on canvas
48 x 36 in. (121.9 x 91.4 cm)

"The idea about art as a way of life,
it's really a way of not dying
before you do. Not being jaded.
I have felt in my life that
the area of my nourishment,
my learning, my enlightenment,
all these things were in my art.
Maybe that's romantic—
but it's true."

William Brice
Los Angeles Herald Examiner
April 20, 1984

EXHIBITIONS
& COLLECTIONS

WILLIAM BRICE

1921	Born New York, New York
1937–39	Cumnock School for Expression and Chouinard Art Institute, Los Angeles, California
1939–40	Art Students League, New York, New York
1940–42	Chouinard Art Institute and Otis Art Institute, Los Angeles, California
2008	Died Los Angeles, California

Solo Exhibitions

2010 *William Brice: Selected Drawings 1960–1985,* L.A. Louver, Venice, California

2009 *William Brice: Drawings and Paintings,* Museum of Art,
San Jose State University, San Jose, California

1998 *William Brice,* L.A. Louver, Venice, California

1993 *William Brice: Works on Paper, 1982–1992,* Grunwald Center for the Graphic Arts,
University of California, Los Angeles

1990 *William Brice: Notations 1982,* Los Angeles County Museum of Art,
Los Angeles, California

William Brice: Watercolor Paintings, L.A. Louver, Venice, California

1989 *William Brice: Drawings,* L.A. Louver, Venice, California

1986 *William Brice: A Selection of Painting and Drawing, 1947–1986,*
Museum of Contemporary Art at the Temporary Contemporary, Los Angeles, California

traveled to: Grey Art Gallery and Study Center, New York University, New York, New York

1985 *William Brice,* Tyler Gallery, Temple University, Philadelphia, Pennsylvania

1984 *William Brice: Recent Work,* L.A. Louver, Venice, California

William Brice: Paintings and Pastels, Robert Miller Gallery, New York, New York

1983 *William Brice Paintings and Drawings,* Smith Andersen Gallery,
Palo Alto, California

1981 *William Brice: Drawings,* California State University, Dominguez Hills, California

1980 *William Brice,* Robert Miller Gallery, New York, New York

William Brice: Drawings, Mary Porter Sesnon Art Gallery, University of California, Santa Cruz

1978 *William Brice: Paintings and Drawings,* LAICA (Los Angeles Institute
of Contemporary Art), Los Angeles, California

William Brice: Recent Paintings and Drawings, Nicholas Wilder Gallery, Los Angeles, California

William Brice Drawings, Peppers Art Gallery, University of Redlands, Redlands, California

1976 *William Brice: Paintings and Drawings,* Charles Campbell Gallery, San Francisco, California

1975 *William Brice: Drawings,* Hancock College Art Gallery, Santa Maria, California

William Brice Drawings, Orange Coast College Art Gallery,
Orange Coast College, Orange, California

1968 *William Brice Drawings,* Cowell College Art Gallery,
University of California, Santa Cruz

William Brice: Recent Work, Landau-Alan Gallery, New York, New York

1967 *William Brice: Selection of Drawings 1955–1966,* The Art Gallery,
University of California, San Diego

traveled to: Santa Barbara Museum of Art, Santa Barbara, California
San Francisco Museum of Modern Art, San Francisco, California,
Dallas Museum of Art, Dallas, Texas
Colorado Springs Fine Arts Center, Colorado Springs, Colorado

1966   *William Brice Recent Work,* Felix Landau Gallery, Los Angeles, California

1964   *William Brice,* The Alan Gallery, New York, New York

1962   *William Brice: Drawings, Lithographs and Etchings 1961–1962,*
Frank Perls Gallery, Beverly Hills, California

1961   *The Drawings of William Brice,* Esther Bear Gallery, Santa Barbara, California

       William Brice, The Alan Gallery, New York, New York

1960   *William Brice,* Frank Perls Gallery, Beverly Hills, California

1958   *William Brice: Paintings, Watercolors, Drawings from 1946–1958,*
Santa Barbara Museum of Art, Santa Barbara, California

1956   *William Brice: Recent Drawings,* Frank Perls Gallery, Beverly Hills, California

       William Brice: Recent Drawings, The Alan Gallery, New York, New York

1955   *William Brice,* Frank Perls Gallery, Beverly Hills, California

       William Brice: Paintings and a Group of Drawings, The Alan Gallery, New York, New York

1950   *New Watercolors by William Brice,* Frank Perls Gallery, Beverly Hills, California

1949   *William Brice,* Downtown Gallery, New York, New York

1947   *Paintings by William Brice, Los Angeles,* Santa Barbara Museum of Art, Santa Barbara, California

Selected Group Exhibitions

2007   *Day and Night,* L.A. Louver, Venice, California

2002   *Drawings,* Hunsaker/Schlesinger Fine Art, Santa Monica, California

2001   *Chouinard: A Living Legacy,* Oceanside Museum of Art, Oceanside, California

traveled to: Kruglak Gallery, Mira Costa College, Oceanside, California
Boehm Gallery, Palomar College, San Marcos, California

1995   *Fifteen Profiles: Distinguished California Modernists,*
Fresno Art Museum, Fresno, California

1993   *Drawings III,* Koplin Gallery, Santa Monica, California

1992   *Drawings II,* Koplin Gallery, Santa Monica, California

Painters on Press: Recent Abstract Prints, Madison Art Center, Madison, Wisconsin

1991   *Drawings I,* Koplin Gallery, Santa Monica, California

1989   *Pastoral,* Crown Point Gallery, New York, New York

1987   *Artists Who Teach: Faculties from Member Institutions of the National Association
of State Universities and Land-Grant Colleges,* Federal Reserve Fine Art Program,
Federal Reserve Board, Washington, D.C.

Contemporary Art from The Douglas S. Cramer Collection,
The Douglas S. Cramer Foundation Gallery, Los Olivos, California

Teaching Artists: The UCLA Faculty of Art and Design,
Wight Art Gallery, University of California, Los Angeles,

1985   *Sunshine and Shadow: Recent Painting in Southern California,*
Fisher Gallery, University of Southern California, Los Angeles, California

Tamarind 25ᵗʰ Anniversary Exhibition, Associated American Artists, New York, New York

Friends and Friends of Friends, Paulo Salvador Gallery, New York, New York

Painting, Drawing and Sculpture: American and European Works on Paper,
Robert Miller Gallery, New York, New York

American/European: Painting and Sculpture, Part II, L.A. Louver, Venice, California

1984 *20ᵗʰ Century American Drawings: The Figure in Context,*
International Exhibition Foundation, Washington, D.C.

traveled The Terra Museum of American Art, Evanston, Illinois,
through Arkansas Art Center, Little Rock, Arkansas
1985 to: Oklahoma Museum of Art, Oklahoma City, Oklahoma
Toledo Museum of Art, Toledo, Ohio
Elvehjem Museum of Art, University of Wisconsin, Madison, Wisconsin
National Academy of Design, New York, New York

Eccentric Images, Margo Leavin Gallery, Los Angeles, California

1983 *The Figurative Mode: Recent Drawings from New York Galleries,*
State University of New York, Cortland, New York

Surreal, Robert Miller Gallery, New York, New York

American/European: Paintings and Sculpture,
L.A. Louver, Venice, California

1982 *L.A. Art: An Exhibition of Contemporary Painting,*
Los Angeles Municipal Art Gallery, Los Angeles, California
Sponsored by Cultural Affairs Department, City of Los Angeles, California

traveled to: Nagoya City Museum, Nagoya, Japan

Domestic Relations, Newspace Gallery, Los Angeles, California

Drawings by Painters, Long Beach Museum of Art, Long Beach, California

traveled to: Mandeville Art Gallery, University of California, San Diego
Oakland Museum of California, Oakland, California

Drawings and Illustrations by Southern California Artists Before 1950,
Laguna Beach Museum of Art, Laguna Beach, California

1981 *Los Angeles Prints 1883–1980,* Los Angeles County Museum
of Art, Los Angeles, California

Decade: Los Angeles Painting in the Seventies, Art Center College of Design, Pasadena, California

Southern California Artists, 1940–1980, Laguna Beach Museum of Art, Laguna Beach, California

California: A Sense of Individualism, L.A. Louver, Venice, California

Contemporary Artists, Cleveland Museum of Art, Cleveland, Ohio

1980 *Portraits and Palettes,* Los Angeles County Museum of Art, Los Angeles, California

The Mask and Metaphor, Craft and Folk Art Museum, Los Angeles, California

1979 *Selections from the Frederick Weisman Company Collection of California Art,*
Corcoran Gallery of Art, Washington, D.C.

Related Figurative Drawings, Hansen Fuller Goldeen Gallery, San Francisco, California

1977 *Artists at Work,* Los Angeles County Museum of Art, Los Angeles, California

California Figurative Painters, Tortue Gallery, Santa Monica, California

Group Show, Charles Campbell Gallery, San Francisco, California

1976 *Painting and Sculpture in California: The Modern Era,*

San Francisco Museum of Modern Art, San Francisco, California

traveled to: National Collection of Fine Arts, Smithsonian Institution, Washington, D.C.

Private Images: Photographs by Painters, Los Angeles County Museum of Art, Los Angeles, California

1975   *18 UCLA Faculty Artists,* Frederick S. Wight Gallery,
University of California, Los Angeles

7ᵗʰ Annual Printmaking West, Utah State Institute of Fine Arts, Logan, Utah

1974   *Painting: Color, Form and Surface,* Lang Art Gallery, Scripps College, Claremont, California

1973   *Californians collect Californians,* Henry Weinburger Auditorium, Los Angeles, California

1972   *California: Selections from the Permanent Collection of the Palm Springs Desert Museum,*
Art Gallery of Greater Victoria, Vancouver, British Columbia, Canada

Two Decades of Art Museum Council Gifts, Los Angeles County Museum of Art, Los Angeles, California

1971   *Tamarind: A Renaissance of Lithography,* International Exhibitions Foundation, Washington, D.C.

traveled   Arkansas Arts Center, Little Rock, Arkansas
through   William Marsh Rice University, Houston, Texas
1973 to: Fort Lauderdale Museum of Art, Fort Lauderdale, Florida
Munson-Williams-Proctor Institute, Utica, New York
Indiana University Art Museum, Bloomington, Indiana
Colorado Springs Fine Arts Center and Taylor Museum, Colorado Springs, Colorado
South Dakota Memorial Art Center, Brookings, South Dakota
Hopkins Center Art Galleries, Hanover, New Hampshire
Mankato State College, Mankato, Minnesota
Cheney Cowles Memorial Museum, Spokane, Washington
Princeton University, Princeton, New Jersey
Baltimore Museum of Art, Baltimore, Maryland

1970   *Drawings by Nine West Coast Artists,* The Museum of Art, University of Kansas, Lawrence, Kansas

1969   *American Drawings of the Sixties: A Selection,*
New School Art Center, New School for Social Research, New York, New York

The Institute of Creative Art, The Art Galleries of University of California, Santa Barbara
and La Jolla Museum of Art, La Jolla, California

traveled to: Fresno Art Center, Fresno, California
E.B. Crocker Art Gallery, Sacramento, California
Oakland Museum of California, Oakland, California
Grady Gammage Auditorium, Arizona State University, Tempe, Arizona

Prints and Drawings, Art Unlimited, San Francisco, California

Tamarind: Homage to Lithography, Museum of Modern Art, New York, New York

Second National Invitational Exhibition: Drawings, University of Wisconsin, Green Bay, Wisconsin

1967   *3ʳᵈ Biennial National Invitational Drawing Exhibition,* Otis Art Institute, Los Angeles, California

Recorded Images/Dimensional Media, California State College, Fullerton, California

Selected Artists—'67, Des Moines Art Center, Des Moines, Iowa

Seventeenth Exhibition of Southwestern Prints and Drawings,
Dallas Museum of Fine Arts, Dallas, Texas

National Lithography Exhibition, Florida State University, Tallahassee, Florida

1966   *2ⁿᵈ Biennial Invitational Drawing Exhibition,* Otis Art Institute, Los Angeles, California

1965   *Paintings Sculpture Assemblages Drawing,* The Alan Gallery, New York, New York

Portraits from the American Art World, New School Art Center,
New School for Social Research, New York

1964   *Drawings and Watercolors,* Frank Perls Gallery, Beverly Hills, California

From the Ludington Collection,
Dickson Art Center, University of California

1ˢᵗ Biennial Invitational Drawing Exhibition, Otis Art Institute, Los Angeles, California

1963   *Artists of the University of California 1963–1964,*
University of California, Los Angeles

traveled to: University of California, Berkeley
University of California, Davis
University of California, Santa Barbara
University of California, Riverside

Drawing Invitational 1963, Foster Hall Art Gallery, Louisiana State University, Baton Rouge, Louisiana

Annual Exhibition 1963: Contemporary American Painting,
Whitney Museum of American Art, New York, New York

Fourth Annual Californians collect Californians, Henry Weinberg Auditorium, Los Angeles, California

1962   *Fifty California Artists,* Whitney Museum of American Art, New York, New York

traveled to: Walker Art Center, Minneapolis, Minnesota
Albright-Knox Art Gallery, Buffalo, New York
Des Moines Art Center, Des Moines, Iowa

Whitney Museum of American Art Annual Exhibition, New York, New York

Lithographs from the Tamarind Workshop, University of California, Los Angeles

traveled   Achenbach Foundation for Graphic Arts, California Palace of the Legion of Honor, San Francisco, California
through   Reed College, Portland, Oregon
1965 to: Dallas Museum for Contemporary Arts, Dallas, Texas
Marion Koogler McNay Art Institute, San Antonio, Texas
Contemporary Arts Association, Houston, Texas
Des Moines Art Center, Des Moines, Iowa

Walker Art Center, Minneapolis, Minnesota
Art Institute of Chicago, Chicago, Illinois
Washington University, St. Louis, Missouri
Colorado Springs Fine Arts Center, Colorado Springs, Colorado
Santa Barbara Museum of Art, Santa Barbara, California
William Rockhill Nelson Gallery, Kansas City, Missouri
University of New Mexico, Albuquerque, New Mexico
Ohio University, Athens, Ohio
University of Michigan, Ann Arbor, Michigan
Cornell University, Ithaca, New York

Drawing Invitational: 6 X = 48, Louisiana State Art Gallery, Louisiana State University, Baton Rouge, Louisiana

1961   *Dedication Exhibition,* Krannert Art Museum, University of Illinois at Urbana-Champaign, Urbana, Illinois

The Image Retained, Los Angeles Municipal Art Gallery, Barnsdall Park, Los Angeles, California

traveled to: California Palace of the Legion of Honor, San Francisco, California
Fine Arts Gallery of San Diego, San Diego, California

Disegni Americani Moderni, Museum of Modern Art, New York, New York for the IV Festival dei due Mundi, Pallazzo Ancaiani, Spoleto, Italy

traveled to: Bezalel Museum, Jerusalem, Israel

1960   *Fifty Paintings by Thirty-Seven Painters of the Los Angeles Area,* University of California, Los Angeles

traveled to: San Francisco Museum of Art, San Francisco, California
Roswell Museum and Art Center, Roswell, New Mexico
Museum of New Mexico, Santa Fe, New Mexico
Seattle Museum of Art, Seattle, Washington
Marion Koogher McNay Art Museum, San Antonio, Texas

Dallas Museum for Contemporary Arts, Dallas, Texas
Des Moines Art Center, Des Moines, Iowa

1960 Annual Exhibition of Artists of Los Angeles and Vicinity,
Los Angeles County Museum, Los Angeles, California

Arts of Southern California—VIII: Drawing, Long Beach Museum of Art, Long Beach, California

traveled
through
1962 to:
Dallas Public Library, Dallas, Texas
Everhart Museum, Scranton, Pennsylvania
Columbia Museum of Art, Columbia, South Carolina
Georgia Museum of Art, Athens, Georgia
Columbus Museum of Arts and Crafts, Columbus, Georgia
Eastern Illinois State College, Charleston, Illinois
Historical Society of Montana, Helena, Montana
Art Center of La Jolla, La Jolla, California
Texas State College for Women, Denton, Texas
University of Nebraska, Lincoln, Nebraska

1959   *Eleven Artists of the Art Department Faculty,* University of California, Los Angeles

The Maitland Collection, University of California, Los Angeles

1958   *1958 Annual Exhibition of Artists of Los Angeles and Vicinity,*
Los Angeles County Museum, Los Angeles, California

Fresh Paint—1958: A Selective Survey of Recent Western Painting,
Stanford Art Gallery, Stanford University, Stanford, California

3rd Annual Exhibition of Southland Artists,
Marian Hall of Fine Arts, Mount St. Mary's College, Los Angeles, California

Nature in Abstraction: The Relation of Abstract Painting and Sculpture to Nature in
Twentieth-Century American Art, Whitney Museum of American Art, New York, New York

Arts of Southern California—II: Painting, Long Beach Museum of Art, Long Beach, California

1957   *67th Nebraska Art Association Annual Exhibition,*
University of Nebraska Art Galleries, Lincoln, Nebraska

Edward Wales Root: An American Collector, Munson-Williams-Proctor Institute, Utica, New York

22nd Annual Midyear Show, Butler Institute of American Art, Youngstown, Ohio

Art Exhibit, Santa Monica Art Gallery, Santa Monica, California

California Drawings, Long Beach Museum of Art, Long Beach, California

traveled to: Pomona College, Claremont, California

63rd Annual Exhibition, Denver Art Museum, Denver, Colorado

New Work, The Alan Gallery, New York, New York

Vincent Price Collects Drawings, The Oakland Art Museum, Oakland, California

Second Pacific Coast Biennial Exhibition of Paintings and Watercolors,
Santa Barbara Museum of Art, Santa Barbara, California

traveled   California Palace of the Legion of Honor, San Francisco, California
through   Seattle Art Museum, Seattle, Washington
1958 to: Portland Art Museum, Portland, Oregon

20th Century Works of Art, Galleries, University of Illinois, Urbana, Illinois

3rd Annual Invitational Exhibitions: American Drawings and Prints,
University of Utah, Salt Lake City, Utah

1956   *1956 Annual Exhibition of Artists of Los Angeles and Vicinity,*
Los Angeles County Museum, Los Angeles, California

1956 Annual Exhibition: Sculpture, Watercolors, Drawings,
Whitney Museum of American Art, New York, New York

Recent Drawings, USA, Museum of Modern Art, New York, New York

16ᵗʰ Annual Exhibition of the Society for Contemporary American Art,
Art Institute of Chicago, Chicago, Illinois

62ⁿᵈ Annual Exhibition for Western Artists, Denver Art Museum, Denver, Colorado

Pacific Coast Art: United States' Representation at the III Bienal de São Paulo,
San Francisco Museum of Art, San Francisco, California

traveled to: Colorado Springs Fine Arts Center, Colorado Springs, Colorado
Walker Arts Gallery, Minneapolis, Minnesota
Cincinnati Art Museum, Cincinnati, Ohio

A National Exhibition of Contemporary Arts of the United States, 1956,
Los Angeles County Fair Association, Pomona, California

1955 *III Bienal de São Paulo,* Pavilion of the Nations,
Museo de Arte Modera, São Paulo, Brazil

Exposição Norte Americana de III Bienal de São Paulo,
Galeria Ibeu, Instituto Brazil-Estados Unidos, Rio de Janeiro, Brazil

1ˢᵗ Pacific Coast Biennial Exhibition of Paintings and Watercolors,
Santa Barbara Museum of Art, Santa Barbara, California

traveled to: California Palace of the Legion of Honor, San Francisco, California

1954 *Le Dessin Contemporain Aux Etats-Unis,* Musée National d'Art Moderne, Paris, France

1953 *Four American Painters,* Santa Barbara Museum of Art, Santa Barbara, California

traveled to: M.H. de Young Memorial Museum, San Francisco, California

1952 *National Painting Exhibition,* Art Institute of Chicago, Chicago, Illinois

Metropolitan Museum of Art National Exhibition, New York, New York

5ᵗʰ Annual Exhibition of Contemporary American Painting,
Palace of the Legion of Honor, San Francisco, California

1951   *7ᵗʰ Annual City of Los Angeles Art Exhibition,*
Department of Municipal Art of the City of Los Angeles, Los Angeles, California

1950   *Recent Acquisitions,* Museum of Modern Art, New York, New York

145ᵗʰ Annual Exhibition, Pennsylvania Academy of the Fine Arts, Philadelphia, Pennsylvania

Young American Artists, Metropolitan Museum of Art, New York, New York

1950 Annual Exhibition of Contemporary American Sculpture, Watercolors and Drawings,
Whitney Museum of American Art, New York, New York

Works by Newly Elected Members and Recipients of Honors,
American Academy and National Institute of Arts and Letters, New York, New York

6ᵗʰ Annual City of Los Angeles Art Exhibition, Department of Municipal Art
of the City of Los Angeles, Los Angeles, California

4ᵗʰ Annual Exhibition of Contemporary American Painting,
Palace of the Legion of Honor, San Francisco, California

1949   *Southern California 1948,* Modern Institute of Art, Beverly Hills, California

Drawings of Modern Masters, Yale Art Gallery, New Haven, Connecticut

1949   *Annual Exhibition of Contemporary American Sculpture,* Watercolors, and Drawings,
Whitney Museum of American Art, New York, New York

California Centennials Exhibition of Art, Los Angeles County Museum,
Los Angeles, California

The Annual Exhibition: Watercolors, Prints, Drawings, Miniatures,
Pennsylvania Academy of the Fine Arts, Philadelphia, Pennsylvania

Painting in the United States, 1949, Carnegie Institute, Pittsburgh, Pennsylvania

Exhibition of Drawings: Old Masters and Modern,
Scripps College, Claremont, California

1949 Annual Exhibition of Contemporary American Painting,
Whitney Museum of American Art, New York, New York

1948	*10th Annual Artists West of the Mississippi,* Colorado Springs Fine Arts Center,
Colorado Springs, Colorado

1948 Annual Exhibition of Artists of Los Angeles and Vicinity,
Los Angeles County Museum, Los Angeles, California

8th Annual Spring Purchase Exhibit, Springfield Museum of Fine Art,
Springfield, Massachusetts

Painting in the United States, 1948,
Carnegie Institute, Pittsburgh, Pennsylvania

1948 Annual Exhibition of Contemporary American Painting,
Whitney Museum of American Art, New York, New York

1947	*1947 Annual Exhibition of Artists of Los Angeles and Vicinity,*
Los Angeles County Museum, Los Angeles, California

Painting in the United States, 1947,
Carnegie Institute, Pittsburgh, Pennsylvania

Collections

Addison Gallery of American Art, Phillips Academy, Andover, Massachusetts

Art Institute of Chicago, Chicago, Illinois

Iris & B. Gerald Cantor Center for Visual Arts at Stanford University,
Stanford University, Stanford, California

Carnegie Museum of Art, Pittsburgh, Pennsylvania

Douglas S. Cramer Foundation, Los Olivos, California

Fresno Art Museum, Fresno, California

Grunwald Center for the Graphic Arts, University of California, Los Angeles

Hirshhorn Museum and Sculpture Garden, Smithsonian Institution, Washington, D.C.

Israel Museum of Jewish Art, Jerusalem, Israel

Krannert Art Museum, University of Illinois at Urbana-Champaign, Urbana, Illinois

Laguna Art Museum, Laguna Beach, California

Los Angeles County Museum of Art, Los Angeles, California

Metropolitan Museum of Art, New York, New York

Munson-Williams-Proctor Arts Institute, Utica, New York

Museum of Contemporary Art, Los Angeles, California

Museum of Modern Art, New York, New York

Newark Museum, Newark, New Jersey

Oakland Museum of California, Oakland, California

Orange County Museum of Art, Newport Beach, California

Palm Springs Desert Museum, Palm Springs, California

San Diego Museum of Contemporary Art, La Jolla, California

Santa Barbara Museum of Art, Santa Barbara, California

Sheldon Museum of Art, University of Nebraska-Lincoln, Lincoln, Nebraska

Norton Simon Museum, Pasadena, California

University Art Museum, University of California, Santa Barbara

UCLA Art Collection, Hammer Museum, University of California, Los Angeles

UNM Art Museum, University of New Mexico, Albuquerque, New Mexico

University Art Museum, California State University at Long Beach, Long Beach, California

University of Iowa Museum of Art, University of Iowa, Iowa City, Iowa

University of Michigan Museum of Art, University of Michigan, Ann Arbor, Michigan

Whitney Museum of American Art, New York, New York

Wichita Art Museum, Wichita, Kansas

Credits

This catalogue is published on the occasion of

William Brice: Drawings 1960-1985 → 17 November – 30 December 2010

L.A. Louver, Venice, California

Library of Congress Control Number: 2010936789

ISBN-13 978-0-9843051-0-0 | ISBN-10 0-9843051-0-6

© 2010 L.A. Louver and the Estate of William Brice. All works by William Brice unless otherwise noted. © The Estate of William Brice. All rights reserved. No part of the contents of this book may be reproduced, in whole or in part, without permission from the publisher L.A. Louver.

Photographs:

Page 38 — Large Figure, 1963. Photography by Geoffrey Clements
Page 128 — Kneeling Figure and Window, 1964. Photography by Lee Stalsworth
Page 131 — Photograph by David Hockney, courtesy of the artist and David Hockney Studio, Los Angeles, California
Page 132 — Photography courtesy of Crown Point Press, San Francisco, California
Page 134 — Photograph of Richard Diebenkorn and William Brice in Japan, 1987,
   courtesy of The Richard Diebenkorn Foundation, Berkeley, California
Page 138 — Photograph of "Stark Mock-Walk of Garden Terrace/September 2005/William Brice viewing mockup of Maillol L'Ete" by Gerard Vuilleumier. Digital image © 2005 J. Paul Getty Trust. Photograph of "The Fran and Ray Stark Sculpture Terrace" is courtesy of The J. Paul Getty Museum, and includes the following sculptures: Aristide Maillol, Torse de Dina, 1943, bronze, 48 $^1/_2$ in. x 14 in. x 12 in. © 2010 Artist Rights Society (ARS), New York /ADAGP, Paris; Aristide Maillol, Torse de l'Ete, 1911, bronze (brown patina), 56 in. © Artist Rights Society (ARS), New York / ADAGP, Paris; René Magritte, La Folie Des Grandeurs (Delusions of Grandeur), 1967, bronze, 51 in. x 35 in. x 29-1/4 in. © 2010 C. Herscovici, London / Artist Rights Society (ARS), New York; Barbara Hepworth, Figure for Landscape, 1960, bronze, 103 in. © Barbara Hepworth Estate; Henry Moore, Seated Woman, designed 1958–1959; cast 1975, bronze, Object: H: 203.2 x W: 96.5 x D: 129.5 cm, Weight: 581.5114 kg (80 x 38 x 51 in., 1282 lb.) / Object (base): H: 10.2 x W: 96.5 x D: 129.5 cm (4 x 38 x 51 in.) Gift of Fran and Ray Stark, The J. Paul Getty Museum, Los Angeles. Accession No. 2005.117.3 © The Henry Moore Foundation. All Rights Reserved. / ARS, New York / DACS, London. Photograph of "The Fran and Ray Stark Sculpture Garden" is courtesy of The J. Paul Getty Museum, and includes the following sculptures: Elisabeth Frink, Running Man, 1978, bronze, 77 in. © Frink Estate; Joan Miró, Personnage, 1976–85, bronze, 79 $^3/_4$ in. x 25 $^1/_4$ in. x 11 $^7/_8$ in. © 2010 Sucessió Miró /Artist Rights Society (ARS), New York / ADAGP, Paris; Henry Moore, Bronze Form, 1985, bronze, 168 in. © The Henry Moore Foundation. All Rights Reserved. / ARS, New York / DACS, London; Henry Moore, Seated Woman, 1958, bronze, 75 in. © The Henry Moore Foundation. All Rights Reserved. / ARS, New York / DACS, London; Elisabeth Frink, Horse, 1980, bronze, 108 in. x 108 in. © Frink Estate; Henry Moore, Draped Reclining Mother and Baby, 1983, bronze, 104 in. © The Henry Moore Foundation. All Rights Reserved. / ARS, New York / DACS, London.

Every reasonable effort has been made to identify owners of copyright.
Errors or omissions will be corrected in subsequent editions.

Edited by Lisa Jann
Design by Stefan G. Bucher for 344design.com
Printing by Typecraft, Wood & Jones, Pasadena, California

L.A. Louver
45 North Venice Boulevard
Venice, California 90291
TEl 310 822 4955 | Fax 310 821 7529
www.lalouver.com